THE FINAL TOUCH

Margo Kokko

DECORATIVE GARNISHES

Second Edition

CBI Publishing Company
286 CONGRESS STREET · BOSTON · MASSACHUSETTS 02210

Production Editor: Kathy Savago

Text and Cover Designer: Herb Bowes

Design Coordinator: Richard Hannus

Illustrator: Buzz Gorder

Photographer: Bruce Beauchamp

Compositor: Kingsport Press

Library of Congress Cataloging in Publication Data
Kokko, Margo.
    The final touch.

    1. Cookery (Garnishes) I. Title.
TX652.K53   1982   745.92′4   82–1124
ISBN 0–8436–2258–X   AACR2
ISBN 0–8436–2260–1 (pbk.)

Printing *(last digit):* 9 8 7 6 5 4 3

Printed in the United States of America

"How sweet the lily grows!"

Reproducing nature in a simple elegant manner. The water lilies of dried onion are emphasized by the opening lotus flower with its head above the others.
The lotus is a rutabaga with food coloring added. The pads are fashioned from spinach leaves.

Water lily cut used on page 72; Lotus cut used on page 96.

CONTENTS

Preface   4

Acknowledgments   5

The Final Touch Introduced   7

  Knife Skill   **8**
  Care and Selection of Knives   **14**
  Other Tools and Concepts   **26**
  Know Your *Shun, Kami,* and *Gokun*   **28**
  What Is a Garnish?   **34**

The Final Touch   **47**

  The Art with Universal Appeal   **48**
  Hands   **50**
  Cutting and Slicing Vegetables   **51**
  Cuts for Experiment   **52**
  Additional Cuts and Creations   **57**

The Final Touch Applied   **115**

  Orchestration   **123**
  Helpful Hints   **147**
  Tools of the Art   **148**
  Which Cut to Use for Dinner Tonight?   **150**

Glossary of Japanese Terms   **156**

PREFACE

What prompts a person to write a book? For me, it was my *on*. *On,* as the Japanese use the word, is that which is difficult to express. It is pronounced "own," and the interpretation can be related to the story in *The Magnificent Obsession. On* is a gift given by someone to another person (given by one person to another) who, in turn, is obligated to return a gift of like value to the giver. Value is determined not in dollars but is measured in an intrinsic quality known only to the receiver.

Takahashi-san has been my teacher, giving the fine gifts of his skill, time, patience . . . and the heritage of beauty passed on to him by his people. In accepting lessons from Takahashi-san, I tried at first—with small gifts—to show him the measure of my appreciation.

Years have passed, and I have shared Takahashi-san's gift—demonstrating and discussing this gracious art, yet this attempt did not fulfill my *on*.

The art must be performed to be appreciated. My talking and discussions are an empty shell for the gift, to be of true value, is in the act of performing, enjoying and appreciating this beauty.

Here is my book, with its secret magic for you to share. I am giving my *on* to you.

Margo Kokko

ACKNOWLEDGMENTS

It can be honestly said that this book was written not only for the people who prepare food but also for those who partake of it. So many have contributed over a life-time that it is impossible to count. I would like to name several who worked enthusiastically, for without them this book would not exist.

Kisaburo Takahashi-san, who persevered and patiently taught me the fundamentals and basic skills.

Buzz Gorder, who urged me to "write it all down" and did a superb job of illustrating steps to follow with his art work.

Bruce Beauchamp, who with his camera, "tuned it in a little more."

Tom McPherson, legal counselor, whose poem evokes the inner voice of the book.

Rae Dodge, who was a sounding board as well as a critic and who insisted that I promote usage of the art.

Gene, my husband, who became so involved in the sharing of my *on* that he spent unaccountable hours assisting and giving me encouragement. To him, more than any other, I owe the completion of this book.

Bill Moore's enthusiasm and help.

To the staff of CBI Publishing Company who became involved in the reprinting, doing a thorough editorial job. Thanks to each and everyone.

The Artist In You

Wonder why I believe in the artist in you?
I can see that you see from a different view.
You see colors that must be entirely new,
Inconceivable patterns I wish that you drew.
Could I see through your eyes but a droplet of dew
On the leaf of a weed, the familiar blue
Overhead, or the paintings the autumn winds strew
About randomly everywhere, visions that flew
To the south with the geese, recollected by few,
Disregarded as common, could well stand in lieu
Of the grandest canvases stroked
by the masters. It's true
I believe there's an artist in you—and me, too!

Thomas McPherson

THE FINAL TOUCH INTRODUCED

KNIFE SKILL

You are invited to a unique experience. A banquet! Some may be repulsed—too barbaric—but to others it will be the essence of supreme pleasure. To attend this banquet you will have to take a step back into the history of Japan . . . actually a thousand-year-step to the Heian Period (794–1185) when personal cooking represented *the* manner of entertaining. Cooking was termed "the art of *hōchō*" (knife).

As the honored guest you are to be seated before the *Tokonoma* (an alcove with scroll and flower arrangement). Your shoes are outside the door; you are resting your knees on a tatami mat. Gold, silver, and glassware beautify the table. Amid the rustle of other guests being seated, there is a feeling of anticipation—of suppressed pleasure—for your host is going to demonstrate his knife skill.

Meeting Fate with Dignity

Your host seats himself before the chopping block, which has been hewn from a hardwood tree and placed on leveling bars. The banquet is about to begin.

With a sharp clap of hands, your host announces the entrance of a servant hugging a huge, live carp, which he lays on the chopping block. The fish and the host are the center of attention. With his *hōchō* he strokes the sides of the carp to soothe its spirit, quieting the wriggling fish. Thus mesmerized, the fish is said to be "ready to meet its fate with dignity."

All eyes are riveted on the host who, with a flash of steel, lays back the skin and thinly slices the meat below while still leaving it on the bone. The skin is then replaced and the carp appears as if untouched. Having demonstrated his virtuosity with edged weaponry, the host asks you to participate in a guessing game. From which stream came such a magnificent carp? From which river the water for the tea? From which area of the country the warmed sake you are sampling?

It is serving time. Your host raps the fish on the head or simply drops rice vinegar into its staring eye. The carp responds by literally thrashing itself into convenient bite-sized slices. Quickly you are served these succulent morsels on an oak-leaf plate.* Such a smacking of lips! Guests are expected to relish the dish for its freshness!

In this way *sashimi* (raw fish) was popularized. It truly displays knife skill and even today is considered the choicest morsel to serve one's guests. Your reaction may be "Not for me!" But appreciate, please, the skill of the knife. The knife is the artist's tool as he sculpts vegetables into blossoms to treat both your eyes and your tastes. The Japanese believe the quality and taste of food is determined by the degree of knife skill.

Retracing our steps to the ninth century, we find that Buddhism was influencing the culture of Japan, affecting dietary habits which, in turn, changed the course of history. The Heian Period was an era of great power for the nobles, in particular the members of the Fujiwara family. They established customs and manners which became a written guide for social classes to follow. Their diet consisted mainly of dried fruits, fish, and unpolished rice which they soaked at the table in cups of hot water. They suffered both from malnutrition and indigestion. Physically they

* The custom of using oak-leaf plates is being used today in the Nara Prefecture at the Isi Shrine and Kasuju Shrine.

were weak, due in part to the lack of protein in their diet, as Buddhism forbade the eating of most meats and suggested that the craving for food was vulgar.

In the sixth century Confucius laid down these laws:

Rice affected by weather or turned (by men) must not eat, nor fish that is not sound, nor meat that is high. He must not eat anything discolored or that smells bad. He must not eat what is overcooked, nor what is undercooked, nor anything that is out of season. He must not eat what has been crookedly cut, nor any dish that lacks its proper seasoning. The meat that he eats must at the most *not* be enough to make his breath smell of meat rather than of rice . . . as regards wine, no limit is laid down, but he must not be disorderly!

Common people had no such restrictions on what they ate. From this—common and healthier class of Japanese—came the *Samurai* who were hired as warriors. They found and ate foods from the land, exercised, and were able to overthrow the unhealthy nobility and assume control (Kamakura Period, 1192–1333). Often the *Samurai* were paid for their valor with rice. The proverb goes "The *Samurai* glory in honorable poverty" but they made use of the rice as a portable food which aided them in the prevention of the dread disease of that age, beriberi. The *Samurai* were permitted to wear two swords, whereas the lower class of people were permitted to carry only the short sword. In the tenth century, the straight sword was replaced with the curved weapon. The *Samurai* swords were decorated with black lacquer.

Thanks Be to the Knife!

It was not until the Edo Period (1603–1867), when Japanese cooking attained a high level of perfection, that a class of professional *hōchō*-wielding *(itamae)* chefs appeared. Restaurants had sprung into being. Eating competitions were popular, and those participating consumed unbelievable amounts of sake and food. Cooking schools were established. The word *"itamae"* no longer meant respect of guest for host, but was the title given to the half-sleeve-shirted chef who, with knife, was able to demonstrate his high degree of skill.

Also credited to the ninth century is the establishment of the *hōchō-shiki* (knife demonstration) festival. To understand a knife festival, one must realize that in Japan, on almost *every* day of the year, ceremonies, services, offerings, rites, dances, and prayers testify to the most extraordinary variety of beliefs about the nature of the universe and the ways of influencing the mysterious powers that govern it. The Japanese believe that both living and nonliving things have spirits. Therefore, they give thanks to the knives for their work during the year and thus console the spirit of the knives. This festival, *hōchō-shiki,* takes place each year on January 28. January is devoid of growing vegetables but is called the "harmonious month" and conveys a wish to live in harmony with one another throughout the year. The *hōchō-shiki* festival is performed at the Imperial Palace by the *itamae* chefs who bring with them their favorite knife. Examples of their skill in carving are presented as well as special delicacies.

From Cruelest Weapons to Tools of Art

Confucius reminds us, "If there be a knife of resentment in the heart, the mind fails to act with precision." In working with knives, the *feel* of the knife is crucial. To cut food swiftly into precise pieces, a razor-sharp knife is required. Having used such equipment once, you will never again be satisfied with a dull knife. A knife responds to care as a child responds to love. Cleaned, oiled, and honed, a good knife will not rust; if mistreated or neglected, like a temperamental child, it will rebel finding innumerable ways to defeat and even injure. The knife is the cook's child. Treat it with love. The child will grow "straight" and a straight cut line will become beautiful. "Put your *hōchō* to work with spirit and body straight."

The original *hōchō* was handleless. It had replaced the shell. The master held the cold metal in his hand and used it in a rhythmical motion as if it were an extension of his arm. It was heavy and lacked a keen cutting edge. Its shape resembled our present cleaver. It was expected to perform most any task from killing and skinning animals to thatching roofs. As the demand for better swords grew, so grew the demand for a better knife. Swordsmen wanted a blade that could hold a fine edge and bend without breaking. Perfection was found in the way the Japanese vulcans forged their blades under very low temperatures for long periods of time, folding the metal over and over into various thicknesses before it was finally tempered. Today the use of the knife is determined by its length and blade width.

Although the Japanese perfected the manufacture and use of the *hōchō,* the word *hōchō* was adopted from the Chinese. There once was a famous Chinese cook who could draw, quarter, and then broil, bake, and fry a whole beef with just one knife. His name, it is said, was "Hōchō."

CARE AND SELECTION OF KNIVES

Knife Care

The Japanese would say, "To understand something, start with the tools." Here, the knife is the important tool. The ordinary chore of carving can become an extraordinary art of sculpture by using the right knife. The knife must feel good to the hand for it becomes an extension of your arm as you work. In selecting a knife, hold the knife as you would when using it. Feel the weight, the balance—it is going to work for you (if you let it). Check the tilt of the blade—the length of the cutting edge.

The second general rule is that the knife must be sharp. Most quality knives sharpen and keep an edge. A knife responds to care as a child responds to love. Cleaned, oiled, and honed, a good knife will not rust. If a knife becomes rusty, the rust can be removed with a cork. Dip the cork tip into some moistened cleanser and rub the rust spot. This will remove the rust spot without injury to the knife.

The honing of a fine blade requires a quality "stone." Honing is an art in itself—almost a ritual. Best results are gained if the stone is lightly oiled. Starting at the knife tip, draw the full length of the blade toward you. Repeat several times before turning the blade over and doing the other side. When laid against the "stone," the knife is at a 45° angle. There is no correct amount of strokes to a side as some metals require more honing than others. Test sharpness by trying the edge of the media you are planning to use.

Knives should be washed and cleaned after every use and should never be put through the dishwasher. As you work with this obsolete weapon of war, sublimating its violence to artistic sculpture, you will find beauty in that straight cut line.

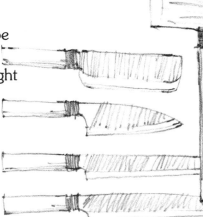

Knife Selection

Where do I find a knife for this art? The answer probably is: in your kitchen. Before buying a knife, check the cutlery you own. How well balanced and how comfortable to your hand is each type of knife you own? You are to *think* of your knife as an extension of your arm. With it you are going to slice, chop, mince, and create beauty. You are going to strive for *rhythm* which you can control. Your knife must feel natural to your hand, and your fingers must not be tense holding it. Using your knife should not tire you.

In purchasing a knife, select one that has a point for piercing the skin surface of vegetables. Some knives have two such points—one being at the "tip end" of the knife, and the other at the "heel" of the knife. Both are useful in starting a clean peel.

Select a knife that has a straight cutting surface. What does this mean? Knives are manufactured to have cutting surfaces. Some knives are made with a curved blade which limits the amount of working (cutting) surface. The working surface extends in either direction from the center of the blade—where the steel edge is straight. This surface controls the evenness of a peel.

Select a knife with which you can slice through a firm vegetable (turnip, rutabaga) with confidence. A cleaver is fine, but a cleaver is not suitable for special cuts. Use a slicing machine if you can control the slicer for the desired thickness. To slice through turnips, rutabaga, or carrots (all firm vegetables) requires a blade that is not flexible, as found in many types of paring knives. Check to see that the blade is not too thin.

Select a knife with a blade wide enough (from cutting edge to top of steel) that you can rest the top of the steel against your curved fingers as you address the item to be cut. Use your chopping block. If you hold the vegetable with curved-under fingers, your fingers help to control the thickness of each cut. The blade may be slanted or held upright depending on the type of cut. Obviously a paring knife would let the knife-blade rest against the fingernails. This method takes practice to gain speed. Rhythmically, fingers guiding, slice the vegetable.

In Japan the knife is looked upon as having a soul. It performs daily for you and must be treated with loving care.

A chef guards the tools of his trade and seldom offers his knife to another. He takes his knife with him from job to job. It becomes a part of his appearance— he wears it—and is seldom seen without his knife. His knife is the most important tool of his trade. Among all the knives he owns for specialty cuts (boning, fish, fruits, and breads) most chefs will possess one knife that is regarded with particular favor and affection. If you are interested in stories, ask a chef about his knife.

It takes understanding to recognize the principle that there is beauty in a clean cut. At first I felt it was quite humorous for Confucius to put in writing *(Analect of Confucius)* "he must not eat what has been crookedly cut." The teaching of basic cuts is neglected. Emphasis has been placed upon recipes rather than on an individual's ability to handle a knife. When confidence in a particular cut is gained, that cut can be performed with rhythm.

Put Your Spirit Before the Block

Itamae chefs are known as "the men before the cutting block"—*ita* meaning block; *mae*, before. This title is reserved exclusively for cooks who prepare formal Japanese dinners. To achieve the rank of *itamae* chef, the individual undergoes forty to fifty years of painstaking training, beginning as an apprentice in his youth around age eleven or twelve. Through watching and practicing, "the men before the cutting block" learn the skills of the knives.

Until only recently, the world of the *itamae* was dominated by the spirit of the craftsmen and by the rules and customs of the prevailing class system. Now this world is changing. Few Japanese today will undertake such strenuous training to become an *itamae*. An aspiring *itamae* was expected to spend at least three to four years in training to assimilate the fundamentals. Then another eight to ten years learning to prepare the soup; to boil, steam, and broil foods to attain a perfection of color and texture each time prepared and to arrange the food on a

plate. Practice was all important. The yoke was rigid. The rules were strict. Rightfully, it should be a proud title. In today's world the *itamae* are being replaced by *chorishi*—one who puts food together—which requires only two years training.

The *itamae* were not restricted in their search for work. In a culture of one-job-for-life, the *itamae* were allowed to seek employment from one restaurant to another throughout Japan to gain experience in ways of knife handling and of different knife shapes. They were required to know the tastes and serving styles peculiar to each region. Their jobs depended on the knowledge that when serving eel in Osaka, the eel is pinned through the eyes to the chopping block. It must be cut across the belly, not down the back as is the custom in Tokyo!

"And lovely is the rose."

This composition was made from the versatile *daikon* and tinted delicately with food coloring. The leaves are natural.

Cut and assembling on pages 97–98.

"Seek roses in December, ice in June."

The combination in this colorful arrangement of the bamboo fan and roses is of carrots and beets with a natural rose tucked in for sheer audacity.

Cut used and assembled on pages 97–98.

Beating the Tongue-Drum

My strong desire to learn vegetable carving drew surprised reaction from those who would locate an instructor for me. Repeatedly I was asked my reasons for wanting to learn, as the Japanese mind questions the motives of all foreigners. My "motives" were simple: to make food more attractive and then to share this knowledge. I had to make this desire clearly understood and not have a "tongue that is too short." After several meetings, in which I was the center of scrutiny, Kisaburo Takahashi-san, Sapporo's 1968 Centennial cook-of-the-year, agreed to become my instructor. At that time, 1969, he was the owner of one crab and five eel restaurants and had a staff of 35 people. He was the sixteenth generation of cooks in his family, which dates its ancestry to the Edo Period (1603–1867). He would not claim the title of "Master Teacher," but he was one of the chefs invited

twice a year to carve at the Imperial Palace, one of the occasions being for the Emperor's birthday.

Takahashi-san told me there were 26 basic designs, but I was to learn to do one correctly—the rose, selected as it represents the symbol of Sapporo's sister-city in America, Portland, Oregon. My lessons were at his restaurant called *Hiyo Setsu No Mon* (Ice and Snow Gate) which was in the heart of Hokkaido's entertainment area. This restaurant had the largest capacity and its name, Ice and Snow Gate, was a memorial nomenclature. During the Russian war, nine Japanese girls volunteered to operate a radio station at the northern-most tip of Hokkaido Island. They built a tower of ice and snow so they could watch the Russians. As the enemy approached, they dispatched the message before they killed themselves. In their honor, the eel restaurant was named.

Our lesson-room was not in the kitchen but in one of the four *tatami* mat serving rooms. The room had a lovely scroll in the *Tokonoma*. The table was low; my shoes were outside the door; my spirit was jubilant. After a half-hour of knee-sitting *(suwaru)*, my back was beginning to ache—I was too tall for the table. Where should I put my feet? I had expected to start by carving a little red radish— I was not prepared for the long, white radish *(daikon)* which he suggested I carve into a rose. I was not even familiar with the vegetable; it was completely foreign to me.

I had nothing but fear, cold gnawing fear for the razor-sharp knife, *hōchō*. This was no ordinary paring knife. It measured some 14″ in length, and the width of the blade was more like a sword. Peel a vegetable with that? Moreover I had to learn to cut on the chopping board and not hold the vegetable above the board. The feeling of the cold steel resting against my curved knuckles sent shivers of apprehension down my aching spine. I did so want to learn.

Takahashi-san spoke no English; I spoke no Japanese. Pantomime was our language. I struggled hard trying to copy his smooth, easy flow of movement. His hands were so beautiful in their performance—mine the personification of awkwardness. Whenever I felt I was beginning to produce a correct cut, I resorted to the American vernacular "okay" emphasizing the word by holding my thumb and second finger tip and repeating "okay?" Later, I learned that the sign I had used seeking approval meant in Japanese "money? money?"

My daily lessons were also a lesson in philosophy of food. I was to learn by watching and through practice. This art of making garden patch vegetables exciting, even glamorous, is like many Japanese traditional arts: the secrets have been handed down from generation to generation through verbal instruction. How very fortunate I was to be a student. Naturally the artist's skilled hands play an essential part in the shaping of material. If you can hold a knife, you can add a touch of romance to any meal.

My teacher described this art of carving as *mukimono—muki* meaning shaped; *mono,* pieces. It is a more advanced skill than *morimono* (stacked pieces). The basic difference in the two is that *morimono* cuts usually are edible, whereas *mukimono* carvings are held together with pieces of bamboo skewers or metal brads. To practice the art of *mukimono* is to carve a seasonal vegetable into flowers, animals, fish, legendary characters, and to arrange them in a symbolic display according to customs. This may be for a certain occasion, state of mind, special event, or to establish a relationship. It is often to honor friendship, love, reverence, joy, sorrow, or even hatred. Each arrangement is telling a story or unfolding a message. Arrangement principles are those pursued by one of the various *Ikebana* schools. Carved vegetables are used instead of flowers. The art offers an exciting challenge to the imagination, and mistakes often elicit new designs. Respectable results can be realized in a very short time. The rewards are plentiful—the horizons are limitless.

OTHER TOOLS AND CONCEPTS

Chopsticks for Contemplation

Appreciating oriental art is like savoring a well-aged bottle of wine. To understand, one must take time to contemplate. As Confucius has put it: "Everything has its beauty. Some persons do not perceive it!" The artist sees universal harmony with man as a part of the scene. In cooking as in painting, there is a visual search for the soul and spirit of nature's shapes, rhythms, and harmonies. Early in life, Japanese children are taught to appreciate how long it takes a single grain of rice to mature. An American might learn the same lesson if he were handed a pair of chopsticks and told to pick up only one grain at a time!

Subtle, hidden inferences are everywhere. Just as silence emphasizes speech, so a single flower is able to express a whole gamut of emotions.

> Behold! A camellia flower
> Spilt water when it fell.

This pursuit of aestheticism permeates every aspect of Japanese life. Witness the simple grace of the tea ceremony; the reverence accorded art treasures; the respect in the depth of the bow when meeting a friend; the harmony in flower arranging. In the subtlety of Japanese culture, even the length of a man's necktie or the width of a woman's kimono sleeve is judged meaningful. Note the *Samurai* guards before a shrine—one with lips open and the other with closed lips. They are uttering the first and last letters of the alphabet. Such is their devotion to duty that from the beginning (ah-h) to the end (m-n-n) they will continue to stand guard.

The wise man, supremely observant, seeks this pure awareness, called *mono no aware,* which can be expressed, if at all, only in poetry:

> Fragile as the dew that falls but
> drop by drop
> And yet this too will pierce
> a stone
> in time.

TAKANO CHOEI

KNOW YOUR *SHUN, KAMI,* AND *GOKUN*

Shun

Integral in the training of a chef is his awareness of the best season and time within the season for each vegetable. His challenge is to make clear both the season and the occasion. This practice is called *shun.* The chef must resort to ingenious ideas to portray this feeling. He is ever cognizant of changes in nature—the yin and the yang—and how to make flavors and textures both stimulate and soothe.

My most vivid experience was one that occurred on my last visit to Ice and Snow Gate. Takahashi-san had prepared a gourmet dinner. The young trainees had carved out of ice a stately swan on whose back were chilled *sashimi* morsels. Attractive small dishes held delicately flavored sauces. This was just the first of many courses to follow. The most dramatically arranged was that of the green *soba* noodles in a large flat bowl. To the eye, they appeared as waves breaking into a hidden shore. On this very warm night, the suggestion of movement and the color hinted of coolness. Imagine the skill it took to make a wet noodle appear so special you feast with your eyes rather than lift a chopstick to disturb the melody.

How very un-American too is this feasting with the eye. Our society is geared to eat-and-run—burgers 'n fries. We are even credited with originating chop suey. The story of this American dish is interesting even though the food lacks beauty. Some gold-miners were having a night on the town in San Francisco. They arrived quite late in Chinatown and demanded that the owner of a small restaurant fix them something to eat. The owner told them the restaurant was closed and there was no food left, but the miners were not to be denied. The frustrated chef retreated to his kitchen. He gathered together all of the day's scraps, scrambled them, added a sauce, and chop suey was born.

In all cooking, the Japanese had experimented extensively to achieve a natural taste. The same materials taste different at different seasons. To cook an exquisite dish one must use the best of materials.

In the practice of *shun* food must be *fresh*. Markets are open at the crack of dawn. Frozen and canned foods both have been a "no, no" because of custom and exorbitant price. Basic sauces call for fresh or dried ingredients. This insistence on freshness once led to an embarrassing occurrence at the Imperial Palace in the preparation of a dinner for a thousand guests. It was the season for crayfish, and these delicacies arrived at the palace kitchen the evening before. The clean-up boy thinking to win favor with the *itamae,* added fresh water to the huge crayfish barrels just before he went home. Inadvertently, he left the water hose in the barrel. The next morning when the chef came to the barrels, there was not a crayfish in sight—they had found temporary freedom by walking the hose! Every crack and cranny became a search area for the missing crustaceans!

Free the *Kami*

To garnish is to ornament. The standard concept is to serve a dish with something bright and savory, as "fish garnished with parsley." To a chef, garnish is a personal expression, a creation to challenge the eye and the appetite. The presentation of the food reveals the attitude and pride of the food handler. To the Japanese the garnish frees the *kami* (essence) of the basic food for appeal to the sense of innate beauty.

Garnish represents a love-marriage between the chef and food—symbolically the joining of two hands. Excitement is created through appearance. As in marriage, harmony can be destroyed if no interest is shown. A successful marriage relationship cannot be attributed to one thing nor can garnish be limited to a sprig of parsley. In this marriage, the garnish is the personal touch and thought that is involved in displaying the food to suggest it was done with love. It is this love that transforms the mundane. Love is reflected in what is served and how it is served to the recipient for his full enjoyment. Care and thought, as well as pride, are members of this concept. The simplest task of slicing a vegetable can be one of perfection.

A true food entrepreneur employs only people who enjoy working with food. A happy atmosphere follows. Dining is anticipated as a symbol of the good life.

The person served enjoys feeling pampered and important. The simple act of serving a plate is special: the salad crisp on an ice-cold plate with a fork that is cool to the touch; the bread rolls, aromatic, served hot; the food separated to display color and shape.

Under Cherry-trees
  soup, the salad,
Fish and all . . .
Seasoned with petals

BASHO

A very special compliment is to have invited guests sit and savor the appearance: "It is too pretty to eat." To destroy beauty has the effect of hesitation on the part of the members served. Most guests try to preserve the beauty of the plate by eating around the outside edge first or carefully lifting a morsel without disturbing the picture. There is a happy, expectant feeling—delight.

Let Your *Gokun* Work for You

The fun of eating-out in Japan is in watching the chef. Many of the dishes are still being prepared before your eyes, almost as it happened in the ninth century. The chef, as a true artisan and with the flare of an actor, performs his art before a captive audience. You are fascinated by his dexterity with his knife; you are tempted by the colorful arrangement of the vegetable tray; your curiosity is provoked by the aroma. As the chef goes into action, you are transfixed by every movement; and your mouth anticipates the feast. The chef is tempting your *gokun*—the appeal of food as measured by the five senses. Here we become a part of the teachings of Buddhism at work. Each dish must appeal first to the eye, in the beauty of the arranged food; next to the smell, in the various sauces and seasonings at work; then to the ear in the sounds of preparation; touch and texture are next; and, last of all, taste.

As the tea ceremony portrays the spiritual effect of moistening a dry life, so the prayer of the cook becomes the harmony of opposites: light and dark, sweet and sour, alive and dead—the joining of two hands. Soft, smooth dishes will be complimented by crisp, crunchy ones. Light foods will be enhanced by dark accents. We are witness to the yin and yang—to an awareness of nature and how its basic elements, ingredients, affect our well-being.

You Eat What You Want to Become

Closely interrelated are foods and medicines. If you were suffering from a fever, you would eat foods that were cool. In winter you would choose foods that were warming. Tea, introduced from China in the ninth century as medicine, is said to aid digestion and dissolve fat. Herb teas are the miracle workers. A nation believing that sickness is caused by an imbalance in the body (yin and yang) uses certain foods and herbs to restore health. By 1500 A.D. herbalists had compiled a list of 2000 drugs and 8000 prescriptions:

ginseng root	envigorating tonic for anemia, depression, colds, rheumatism, asthma and emotional illnesses
cinnamon tree bark scrapings	for upset stomach
dried corn cob	for baby's colic
dried sea horses	for skin disorders
lizard tails	for sexual strength and vigor
chrysanthemum blossoms	general tonic and purgative
dried frog skin	for heart stimulant
cayenne pepper	to open blood vessels
garlic	for purgative

If you have the flu, try a potage of boiled sweet potato and mustard greens! Dramatic in its color impact! I tried it on my mother-in-law—she loved the sweet potato but left the greens! This use of natural foods and combinations of natural materials is a form of medicine called *kampo* which had its origin some 2000 years ago. One of its characteristics is that it has its best effect when it tastes and smells good. As soon as the medicine begins to taste or smell strange, or sits heavy on the stomach, the administration is stopped.

WHAT IS A GARNISH?

In viewing a piece of art we are aware of the harmony of opposites. Viewing food in this manner initiates a new avenue for self-expression. There are many approaches in the planning of a meal to make this harmony of opposites possible. The total effect is completed with garnishes.

A Garnish Can Be Colorful Table Linens

A world of color and texture is available. Plan your table linens to fit the occasion, season, and type of food to be served. Runners as well as placemats are effective for color. Colorful napkins add accent and interest when arranged in an unusual fold. Experiment.

Robust, hearty meals are dramatized when served with strong colored linens and heavier dishes. Delicate soups, light lunches are complimented by pastels and lighter weight dishes. Use your imagination. You are an artist and here is a delightful area to express your sensitivity.

A Garnish Can Be a Serving Dish

Color contrast is the theme. Experiment with different shaped and different colored dishes when serving a meal. Think color and how the food served will appear in the dish. Food displays best when it is "placed" not "dumped" on a plate. The shape of the container will make a difference in the appearance. By using your imagination you are creating interest which opens conversation.

A Garnish Can Be a Centerpiece

This is a fun project. When time is pressing, use one of your smaller growing plants. Add to the plant, vegetable flowers that are placed on bamboo skewers. For example: shamrock with carrot flowers or primrose with grapefruit-peel flowers. Make your centerpiece attractive from each side envisioned. This centerpiece can denote the season or occasion for which it is being used.

The next alternative is to create a vegetable centerpiece that is to be just that— a centerpiece. These cut "veggies" can be arranged in a favorite *Ikebana* form of a height that permits eye contact with the person across the table. For example: the bell pepper or Chinese cabbage antherium, the onion lotus or water lily, or the tomato-peel rose. The greens for this arrangement can be washed leaves from your yard or garden greens cut into leaf shapes. Make this arrangement ahead of time. When time is not an issue, display your knife skill and fashion the petaled rose, camellia, chrysanthemum, and dahlia. Keep these assembled flowers in ice water until time to place in the arrangement. These assembled flowers can be saved and freshened for use at a later time by placing them in ice water and keeping them in the refrigerator.

Your third choice for a centerpiece is the most exciting. This centerpiece is part of the menu—an appetizer or dessert. For example: a basket of colorful snacking vegetable flowers and for dessert a melon sunflower or rose. Caution should be exercised in selection of a container that is easy to pick up for serving. Guests enjoy being able to select the edible and the amount desired.

> For a lovely bowl
> Let us arrange these flowers . . .
> Since there is no rice.
>
> BASHO

A Garnish Can Be an Additive

Condition yourself to color when working with food. Visualize the appearance of the meal. The additive selected is the agent used to heighten the flavor, to make the food have more eye appeal, and to emphasize the contrast in texture. As an example, when serving any fish, the additive could be lemon. This lemon may be cut in a wedge, slice, or basket, depending upon the amount the host feels is proper. Now to add further color contrast and not interfere with taste, the lemon's cut edge is rolled in paprika, minced parsley or mint, or black sesame seeds. At all times, the additive must appear crispy fresh and natural.

Your kitchen cupboard is filled with additives: eggs, pimiento, cheese, grated carrots, sesame seed, salt, ground pepper, coconut, raisins, lemon, nuts, bacon, parsley, and a host of seasonings. Try using croutons on string beans, stewed tomatoes, or steamed *bok choy*. Marmalades and jelly are colorful toothsomes to add to baked sweet potatoes, carrots, or Brussels sprouts.

A Garnish Can Be a Simple Vegetable Cut

Start with a vegetable, making the same thickness of slice. Notice what happens to the edge of a tray when these slices are placed side by side around the tray. If the slice is large, cut it in half, and then place these half cuts around the edge. Try overlapping the cuts. Try combining a vegetable of contrasting color. Interesting designs can be formed from the sliced cut.

As you start formulating patterns, try placing meats on a tray in the shape of birds, butterflies, or a scene. To develop a "scene," use a combination of meat, fruit, and vegetables to give a complete color range. Sometimes the simplest shape

is the most provocative. Personalize the food you prepare. It has your signature upon it. Plan your menu to be presented with a flourish. Use the N cut daily as well as the *rangiri* (roll) cut. Practice "placing" food versus "dumping." The time spent will be worthwhile.

A Garnish Can Be a Decorative Cut

All cuts of vegetables are decorative when placed in color contrast. The simple slice and dice cuts take no more time to do than the roll cut *(rangiri),* broom, fan cut, or the stylized flower cut. First you must learn how to make these cuts. Each time you work with the cut it will take less time to perform. You did not learn to run before you walked.

Time and money are important to most people. With the *rangiri* cut, which is not to be mistaken for the diagonal cut, it is possible to serve ten people adequately with three baked potatoes! Two stalks of green celery and two carrots are enough for appetizers for a party of ten. There is no more preparation time involved when you know knife skill, and it is more gratifying to spend time cutting vegetables that will be consumed. Leftover vegetables often become a headache to use, and frequently are wasted. Open your world to the visual beauty you can create. Let your family enjoy. Let them be aware of color and texture. Train their eyes and save on your food budget.

Contrast

Garnish, as we have explored, encompasses the total effect that creates beauty—accomplished strikingly through color contrast. Contrast is the common denominator. Contrast emulates the difference between ordinary and exotic. Contrast is so obvious that it is overlooked.

A camellia is a-born.

The delicate carving of the *daikon* accentuates the fragile flower.
Cut on page 103.

"And a butterfly flitted across the field, and all the leaves were calling me."

A *morimono* cut of cold meat slices accentuated by sliced black olives and the delicate green of sliced cucumber. Note red pepper for accents and spinach.

To invite attention, to startle the eye, there must be *contrast*—light with dark, sweet with sour, coarse with smooth, spicy with bland, and even hot with cold. It is a basic rule. The rule does not demand a special knife skill but emphasizes color to gain its purpose. Visualize the excitement a tablespoon of green peas makes to a head of snow-white cauliflower, sesame seeds to bright green asparagus, bright orange peel to vinaigrette beets, or a cheerful twist of lemon peel to pink salmon—all involve color to invite, to tempt desire. Contemplate each dish as to its final appearance. Will an unusual cut add interest? What you serve is a picture. Complete the picture so it has eye appeal.

Contrast does not begin and end with color. Contrast is in the taste—the sweet with the sour, the bland with the spicy, and the coarse with the fine—all of these basic elements are a part of the total effect. Experiment with various foods. Know which vegetables complement each other. Know which spices mellow or heighten flavor. Know the subtlety of wines. Know the fruits that suggest coolness and freshness. This is a learning skill.

"All well and good," you say. "But I'm not artistic. I don't do that much entertaining. I don't have time!" Valid excuses? Yes. Even so, who is willing to say they do not have time to be a caring person? Time to focus on well-balanced meals? Time to eat less but savor more? Time to show love in the daily task of meal preparing and presentation? Time, our most valuable asset, can be directed to presenting food as a superb symphony with a minimum of effort. Be among the enlightened. Dare to present food in an individual manner with beauty. With your food dollar becoming more dear each time you visit the grocery store, express your appreciation of what you have through your knife skill.

> The host said not a word.
> The guest was dumb
> And silent, too, the white chrysanthemum
>
> RYôTA

Buying Vegetables

A market should be more than just a place to buy food. It could be a social event; a recipe exchange; a conglomerate of sights, sounds, and smells of different vegetables and fruits. A hundred different people have a hundred different tastes, but here in the market with its still-life array of raw food, you can become the transforming artist. Select vegetables for freshness, color, and shape.

Some produce even suggests certain designs. When you view a bell pepper, visualize the in-curve of the pepper. Does it not resemble the curved spathe of an antherium? Red peppers are almost the exact color of the antherium. Within seconds, with the aid of a carrot stick as stamin, a lovely flower is born. The out-curves of a Chinese cabbage (Napa cabbage) complement the white antherium. With your knife, cleanly cut the shape from the stalk. The tilt of a small zucchini resembles a boat. The roundness of a turnip suggests the number of petals that can be formed from a single slice, and the *Artist in You* stirs the mental image.

Generally, the firmer the vegetable, the easier it is to design and the longer it will keep. Vegetables can be cut into shapes hours before serving time. Centerpieces can be made well in advance and kept fresh by putting in ice water. Other freshening products as ascorbic acid, lacquer that is sprayed, and *myoban* (a white powder used by the Japanese) are effective. The more firm vegetables will appear fresh for a week if refrigerated and fresh water kept on them. For carving, the *daikon* and the carrot rate high. Each of these two vegetables, when cut into a continuous peel, have a very exquisite pattern that appears as fragile as a flower petal.

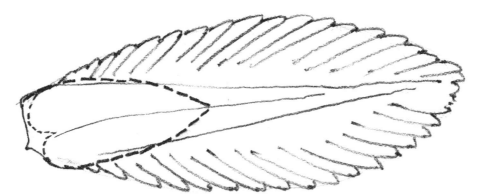

The Great White Radish

The elongated white radish known as *daikon* is perhaps the most versatile vegetable for carving. It is very delicate in flavor. Eaten raw with most fish dishes, it is usually grated. Cooked, it tends to take on the character of the meat or the seasoning. Pickled, it becomes quite tangy. In Japan the radish is consumed daily in many diverse ways.

Daikon means "big root." The size tantalizes! There are 34 varieties of *daikon* produced in Japan. Some of the radishes grow to a length of 5 feet, whereas other types weigh as much as 50 pounds. This big root is a member of the rape family and is a biennial vegetable. It is very rich in vitamin C, diastase, and lysine. Compared to our familiar small red Western radish, it is monstrous. As a working medium, its extreme size, crispness, and ability to assimilate food coloring make it an important tool. The vegetable now appears in most supermarkets, although we are just learning how to use it. The price of the *daikon* in Japan is referred to as a barometer of the economy. One word of caution in selecting a *daikon* is to check to see that it is not pithy but freshly firm.

Check Point

Are your senses awakening to the philosophy of food? There is romance in the kitchen when vegetables are no longer a chore but a delicate harmony of shape, color, and taste. Pick up your favorite knife and slice into the "eye-magination" that follows. The very simplicity of this visual art makes it a *must*. Its tools are available to anyone. If you can hold a knife, you can be an artist conscious of "the final touch."

THE FINAL TOUCH

THE ART WITH UNIVERSAL APPEAL

You are aware of the history of the knife. You are aware, also, of the cultural difference in attitudes toward nature and inanimate objects. Now we are going to show basic cuts to assist you in food preparation. We want you to take pride in creation—freshen up your act—using *any* ordinary knife. We want you to become confident and to practice this ancient art which was coveted for the nobleman's table. When the nobleman's power collapsed, this art did not die. The art remains very much alive today—more people the world over are aware of beauty in food. It is practical and economical for daily use. It is time to learn.

The final touch should be described as knife skill rather than decorative garnishes. The Japanese calligraphy, *mukimono,* translates roughly as "peeled things." This "peeling of vegetables" becomes an acquired skill as the "things" are placed and arranged on a plate. Recognition of the tool (the *hōchō*) for its performance is celebrated each year in the festival on January 28, *hōchō-shiki.* Selected master chefs bring and prepare food at the Imperial Palace. Here the chefs display knife skill in the "peeling and shaping" of food pieces which are then arranged to become a whole within a part—to incorporate in a small space the feeling of the universe. Awe-inspiring? Impossible? Not really. Caring? Yes! The end result challenges the ability to use knife and knowledge effectively.

Instinctively people program their minds to believe that techniques of carving meats are too specialized—boning-out is too difficult and is something you pay the local butcher to do; slicing shapes into various designs and sizes for fresh appearance is too time-consuming. With this type of negative attitude toward basic culinary skills, it is a small wonder that meals appear thrown together. We hesitate to admit we have neglected to learn basic knife cuts. At one time, quantity was the master. In today's world of the good life, quantity has been replaced by eye-appealing quality. The ever-shrinking food dollar demands know-how to keep the good life without sacrificing quality. Knife skill is essential to every household to stretch the food dollar. Strangely enough, knowing how to prepare meals using various cuts saves both money and amount of food required.

One of the measurements of a good chef in Japan is the ability of the chef to know the amount of food each person will consume the moment the customer walks in the door. This, too, is a practiced art. It is important for every restaurant to study what foods are being thrown into the garbage. To avoid loss, perhaps the same food should be presented in a different manner (cut) with proportions not too overwhelming.

Placing food items on a plate has an aesthetic sensitivity. It is an art to suggest abundance when there is scarcity, to suggest a change of season, to reveal beauty in the inanimate—an awareness of nature. Color contrast magnifies beauty. Feeding the soul becomes as important as filling the stomach.

Ah me! I am one
Who spends his little breakfast
Morning-glory gazing

BASHO

Train yourself and those you love to enjoy food through its eye appeal. Small portions, arranged artistically, arouse excitement. One beautifully red-ripe strawberry placed on a sprig of green can suggest an entire field of berries. Savor this seasonal treat to its full enjoyment. Let it become an eating experience worthy of comment. Each season will develop its own culinary specialties. Each individual can enjoy this form of the good life by recognizing the importance of how to display and prepare for finest flavor.

It is here we can practice the penetrating insight of Buddhism—with our *hōchō* we can clear the way for knowledge of the truth. Food is beauty.

HANDS

It is within your hands to accustom yourself with the art of *mukimono*. When it comes to creating, if you feel you are all thumbs, start by holding your fingers together. This simple act of discipling your fingers makes *every* gesture more significant. Your hand acts as a single unit, not as five fingers pointing in all directions. This habit of holding the fingers close together is practiced in all things Japanese. The movement of the hand is confined to a limited space.

Watch a chef. See how he confines his fingers, how he holds a vegetable, and how he exercises safety without being obvious. Watch an *ikebana* instructor arrange flowers. See how he picks up and holds a single flower before placing in an arrangement. Every movement is meaningful without being wasted. Watch any martial artist demonstrate his skill. Every movement is disciplined to present the smallest possible target. The movements are graceful.

You, too, can effectively use your hands as a single unit, keeping you in control. A masterpiece cannot be created through skill alone. It is the care and love you put into your cooking that will blend into an orchestrated whole.

The farmer rose from where he dug and hoed:
A fresh-pulled turnip pointed out my road.

Issa

CUTTING AND SLICING VEGETABLES

The most familiar cuts of vegetables are:

- Circle Cut—sliced thick or thin from end to end. (*Variation:* the circle cuts made into halves and quarter rounds.)

    Wa-giri (round slice)
    Hangetsu-giri (crescent cuts)
    Icho-giri (round slice then quartered)

- Diced Cut—slices made into various sized cubes.

- Strip Cut—slices made into long pieces. (*Variation:* the diagonal slice are strips that are cut at an angle; the julienne cut are very thin strips with diagonal cut)

    Tanzaku-giri (rectangular cut)
    Mijin-giri (mince cut)
    Sengiri (thin strip)

Next is the challenge of using these same familiar cuts in a new way. Examples follow of decorations for salads and hot dishes which may stimulate your creativeness in making patterns. Experiment!

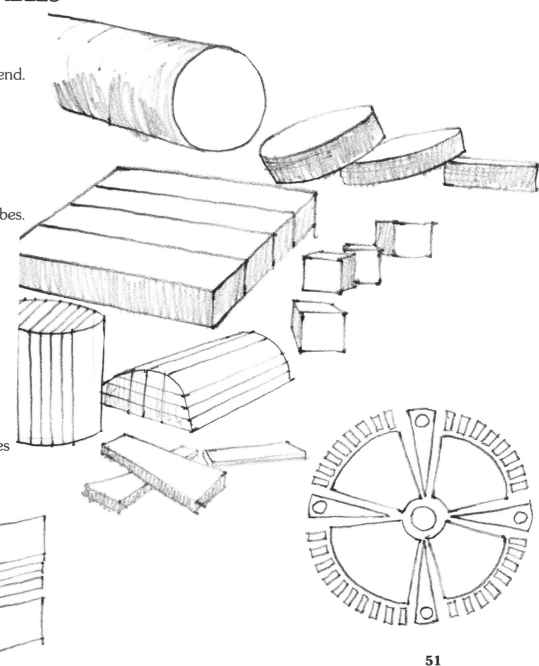

51

CUTS FOR EXPERIMENT

Bark Cut

Firm vegetables are most suitable for this basic cut, which is also called *katsuramuki* (cut in thin sheet).

1 Peel the vegetable and then cut it into a 2" piece.

2 Hold this vegetable piece firmly and thinly peel around as bark peels off a tree. It will take practice to peel a very thin strip that will curl gently. As you gain confidence, you may use a 3" piece which you need for creating a magnolia or large peony.

Roll Cut *(Rangiri)*

This *rangiri* cut is the most important cut described in this book. Tubular vegetables (carrot, parsnip, *gobo,* celery, or asparagus) are ideal for this cut.

1 Peel the vegetable or wash clean.

2 Lay knife almost parallel against vegetable and cut lengthwise a desired length. Cut from top to bottom front edge.

3 *Roll* the vegetable one-third and continue angle-slicing and rolling. Each piece will be its own unique self. This cut is an extreme angle from top of vegetable to the bottom front edge. The rolling of the vegetable each time it is cut makes the cut piece triangular at the center. It is not a diagonal cut *(nanami-giri).*

Baked potatoes cut lengthwise into quarters first and then roll cut should be tried. This cut permits three baked potatoes to serve ten people. This cut is an energy saver when steaming carrots. Its finished shape permits faster cooking because the cut exposes more of the inner fibers to the heat. This cut saves *money*!

Pencil Cut

This cut is best suited for a firm vegetable.

1 Peel the vegetable, leaving it in the shape of a pencil.

2 Start at the root end (pencil tip end) and, using this tip as a pivotal point, thin peel around the tip.

3 These peelings automatically curl and for the final touch can be used individually or intercurled with another peel.

(*Note:* Expect the peel to break as you roll the vegetable but continue peeling until circle is completed. Edges will be fluted. This pencil shell can be filled with mayonnaise, black olives, or other condiments.)

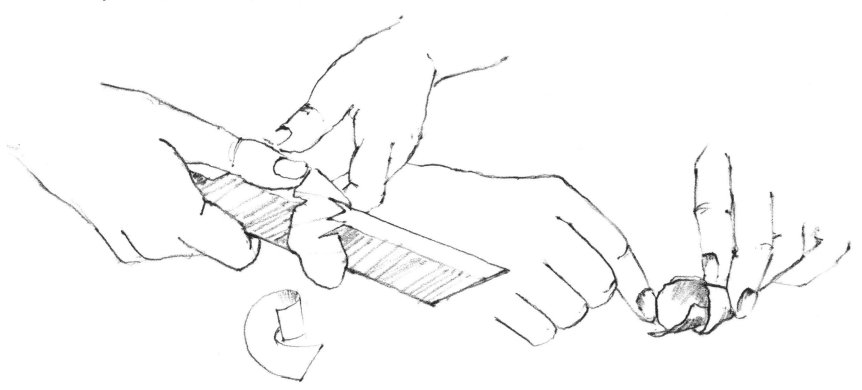

Angle Cut

This cut can be used for a simple carrot garnish.

1 Peel the carrot. Start at the stem end and with your vegetable peeler cut a long strip from top to bottom, *turning* the carrot in your hand as you peel.

2 This peel comes off the carrot at an extreme angle which naturally curls. Place in ice water.

3 If a tighter curl is needed, roll the peel and fasten with a toothpick before putting in ice water.

Curl Cut

This cut is popular for celery, a dainty garnish.

1 Cut the celery stalk into a 2″ piece.

2 Cut this 2″ piece into strips ¼″ wide.

3 Make a diagonal cut 1″ long and repeat this cut. You should be able to get 4 or 5 extreme angle cuts to a side.

4 Place in ice water. This cut will spread and make a very delicate curve with sharp angle spears. This cut loses its zing if the strips are more than ¼″ wide because the spears will not flare.

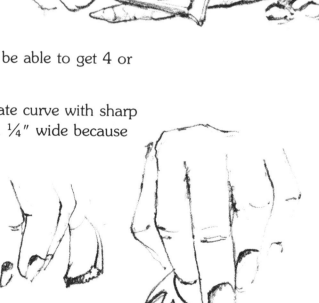

Decorative Spheres

This cut is purely decorative and is a happy final touch to a meat platter. Use an orange, lemon, or grapefruit half.

1 Cut the unblemished orange in half.

2 Remove the fruit cleanly by separating the fruit from the white membrane with the tip of your knife.

3 Slip your thumb tip into this separating cut. Using your thumb as a digger, ease the fruit away from the shell. Lift out.

4 You are going to cut circles, triangles, and half-moons in the empty fruit shell. Use the tip of your knife. Cut cleanly through the shell. Cuts can be made at random.

This is an unusual as well as colorful garnish.

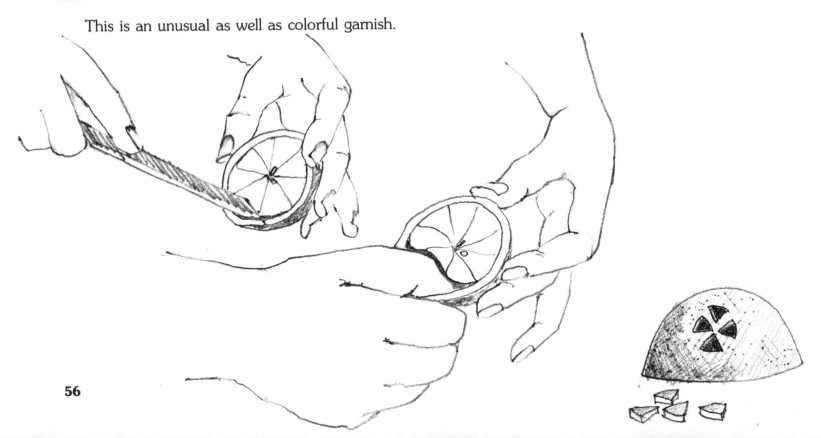

ADDITIONAL CUTS AND CREATIONS

Broom Cut

This cut is great for snacks using celery and carrots.

1 Cut a 2″ piece of selected vegetable and slice thin lengthwise.

2 Start about ½″ from the top end and with tip of knife cut lengthwise into thin strips.

3 Place the cut piece in ice water so the strips will spread.

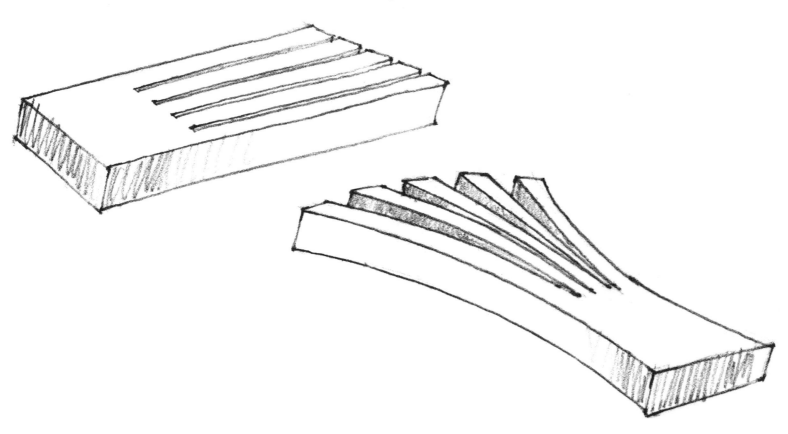

Fan Cut

Use this design for pickles or vegetables that have been parboiled.

1 Using a whole pickle, start ½″ from the stem end and slice the entire pickle into lengthwise strips.

2 Arrange on tray in shape of fan by laying the cut pickle on the tray with cut edges upright.

3 Press down *sharply* on the uncut stem end and *rotate* a quarter turn.

This combined pressure and turn spreads the cut into a fan.

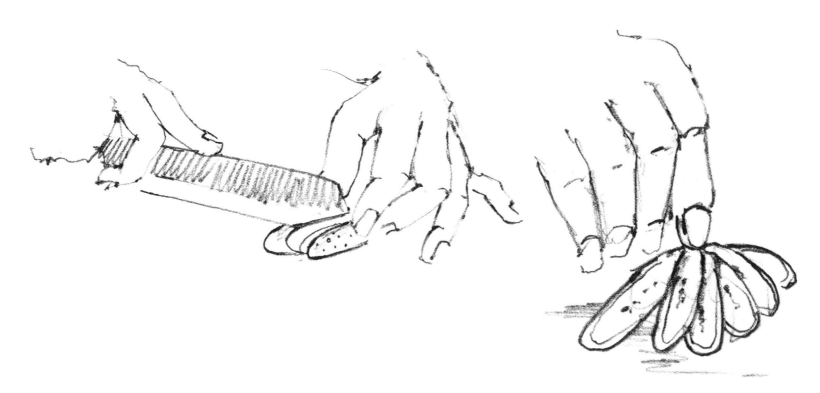

An Imperial Flower—the Chrysanthemum.

Here individuality was given to one flower, the tinted *daikon,* to show the effectiveness of a simple single flower for a centerpiece.

Cut on page 104.

"The rose that lives its little hour
Is prized beyond the sculptured flower."

Exciting with its color impact is the tomato peel that winds itself into a rose with
center of lemon peel.

Cut described on page 94.

Bird Cut

This fun project for any table is usually made from a firm vegetable. Potatoes, turnips, and *daikon* are suitable. The *daikon,* however, can easily be colored.

Follow the detailed drawings shown here. *Feel* what you are doing. Cut slowly. For the eye of the bird either use food coloring and paint it in or use a brad with a larger head. Check your proportions.

If you wish to serve the bird as an edible rather than as a decoration, complete the first five steps of the cut, then slice.

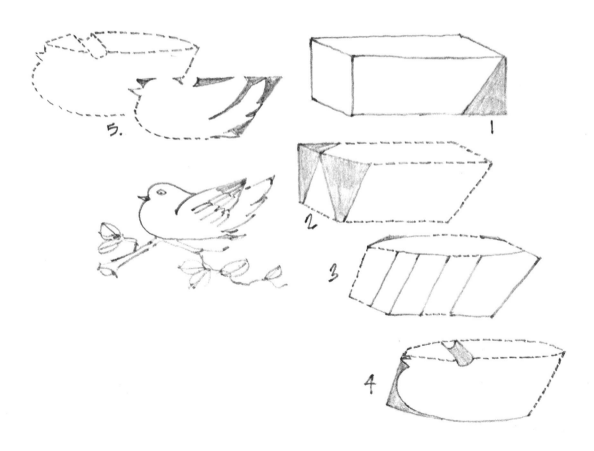

Bowl Cut

This cut adapts itself to fruits, such as oranges and melons of all types, as well as eggplant, squash, and tomatoes.

Orange

Use a large orange and simply slice it in half, which will give you two bowls.

1 Remove the fruit cleanly by separating the fruit from the white membrane with a knife tip.

2 Using your thumb tip, continue to separate the fruit from the shell until you can lift the fruit out.

3 If the fruit adheres to the center membrane, use a grapefruit knife and cut the fruit free. Remove.

4 Slice a thin piece from the bottom of the bowl so the orange sits level.

Orange V

Use a large orange.

1 Angle your knife and cut V shapes around the middle of fruit. These V's should be about ½" in length.

2 When you have cut completely around the orange with V's, reinsert your knife and cut to center, following the same pattern of the original cut. Pull apart.

3 Remove the fruit, following steps 1, 2, 3, and 4 for the Orange Bowl.

Fish Cut

Cut this simple fish from a *daikon*. Follow the diagram, checking your proportions.
Use food coloring. Make your own variety of fish.

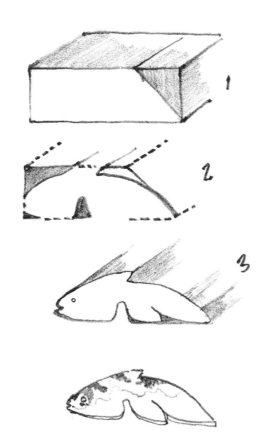

Cup Cuts

Best for lemons, tomatoes, and small squash. The procedure is much the same as for bowl cuts except

1 Slice off about ¼ of the length of the lemon. As your lemon is small, it is more time-consuming to remove the fruit.

2 Follow steps 1, 2, 3, and 4 for the Orange Bowl.

Radish Cuts

This photo illustrates a ten year old girl's first attempt with a knife.

Basket with Handle

Use melons of all types and large fruits.

1 The stem end of the fruit is used as a base and made to stand level. Do first, then turn fruit over.

2 At about ⅓ of the fruit height, insert a skewer through the fruit. This placement of skewer determines how long a handle you will make.

3 Make a mental picture of the center and proceed by making a cut on either side of the center—minimum of ¼″ from center. Slice to depth of skewer. This will give you a handle width approximately ½″.

4 Following the skewer line, cut horizontally from the outer edge toward the center (handle) and remove this triangular piece.

5 Repeat step 4 and do the opposite side.

6 Remove the fruit first from the basket. Success will be yours by following steps 1, 2, and 3 for the Orange Bowl.

7 Remove the fruit from the handle *last* as it enjoys the support of the fruit while you work with the basket.

Boat Cuts

Zucchini Boats

Choose a small zucchini that has the suggestion of a tilt to one end.

1 Make the base level.

2 Parboil for one full minute and quickly douse in ice water to keep the color brilliant.

3 Working from the bottom to the stem end, thinly slice a piece the length of the zucchini, being careful not to break the slice as this elongated piece becomes the mast for the boat. Slice up to 1″ from the stem end.

4 Lift the attached slice upright.

5 Put a bamboo skewer through the slice from *top* to *bottom*. The skewer should sit firmly into the zucchini. If it is too tall for a mast, snip off the end.

6 Using your knife tip, lift out the meat below the slice cut. A small spoon may be of assistance to you here depending on how deep you want your boat. Set the meat aside to be used later if desired.

7 Your boat is ready for its flag, which can be fashioned from a lemon, green pepper, or orange triangle.

Cucumber Boats

These are cut in half lengthwise.

1 Level the base.

2 Scoop out the pulp.

3 Refill the boat with tartar sauce.

Pineapple Boats

These are cut in half lengthwise, down through the leaves and fruit. If the fruit is exceptionally large, the halves are made into quarters.

1 Remove the fruit and core.

2 Cut the pineapple into bite-sized pieces and combine with other colorful fruit.

Protena

This is a showy African flower.

1 Use a large, red bell pepper that is without blemish.

2 From the tip to the stem end, cut many thin slices to within 1″ from the heavy stem end.

3 Wash out the loose seeds.

4 Let stand in ice water for one-half hour. The pepper flares easily.

5 Smooth off stem end and with heavy skewer, start from the inside of the pepper, through the seed-ball, and secure to a firm, red rhubarb stalk. Showy! The seed-ball center is attractive in itself.

   (*Note:* Small hot peppers can be used in like manner. Their colors are unusual. Their seeds are hot!)

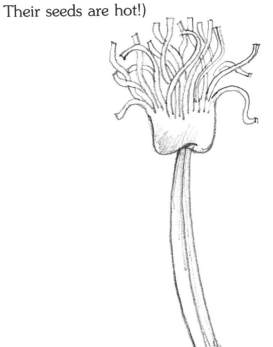

Mushrooms are Fun

Pick fresh mushrooms with stems. Put your imagination to work.

1 Make dainty angle slices on the top of the mushroom.

2 Remove the pieces exposing the white meat of the mushroom.

(*Note:* An easy way to clean mushrooms is to place in a plastic bag of water to cover the mushrooms and 1 tablespoon vinegar. Swish the mushrooms around in this vinegared water, and then rinse clean.)

Rabbit

You might call this cut "Grandma's delight" for it has instant child appeal. Made from turnips or *daikon,* with ears lightly pinked on the inside, this cut is attractive. Follow the diagram. Check your proportions.

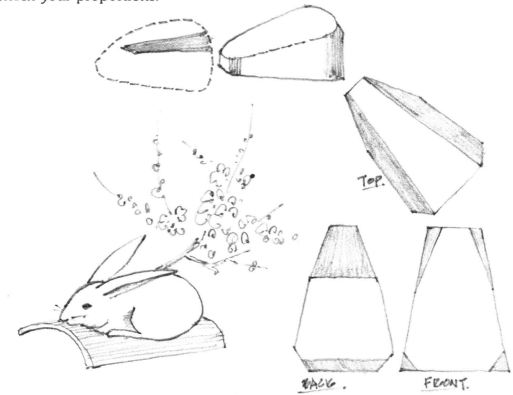

TOP.

BACK.   FRONT.

Working with Onions

Here are two cuts to be used with dried onions. Any variety may be used, purple, yellow, or white. You will find that a cold onion will not make you cry as you cut it. If the onion is especially strong, put it under cold running water, and that too will keep the tears from starting.

Dried onions make a fairly large flower, a chrysanthemum or lotus. If you are planning to serve the onion with your meal, boil the onion quickly after you have peeled it and sliced or dice cut it in the fashion you want. Boil the onion for a full three minutes. Place it under cold water. About 10 minutes before serving time, put the boiled onion into the oven to heat through and serve. Lovely on a meat platter.

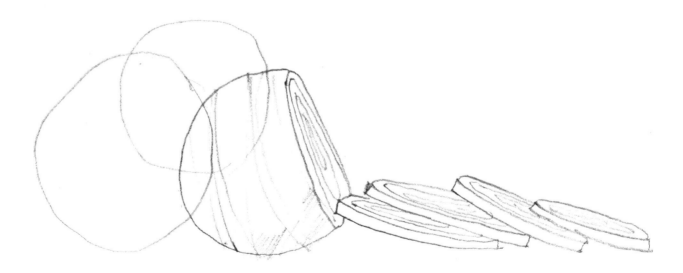

Chrysanthemum Dice Cut

This is known as *kikka-kabu* cut (cut like chrysanthemum flower).

1 Peel the onion. Cut off the root end so that it will sit evenly.

2 About ½″ from the root end, run a skewer completely through the onion from N to S.

3 Run another bamboo skewer from E to W crossing over the first skewer. These are your guidelines for cutting.

4 Slice the onion, in even slices, from the top to the skewer.

5 Turn the onion, and repeat step 4 in the E to W direction.

6 Put in ice water, after removing skewers.

7 Add a drop of yellow food coloring to the water to make the flower resemble the Imperial flower of Japan.

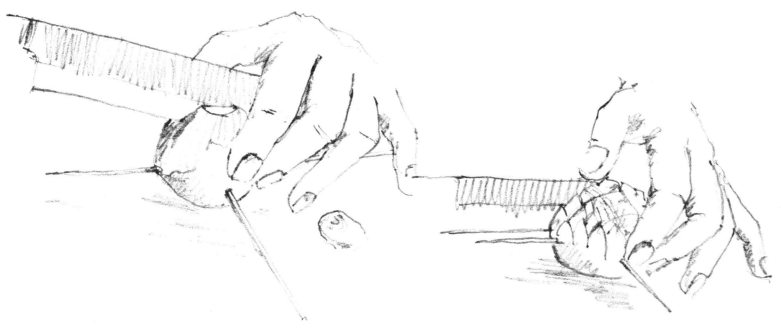

Chrysanthemum Lotus Cut

1 Peel the onion. Cut off the root end for an even base.

2 With skewers, repeat steps 2 and 3 for the dice cut.

3 Now divide the onion into sixteen equal parts by first cutting the onion in half, then quarters, and so on.

   (*Option:* Here you may boil the onion for three minutes and drop it in cold water, or, use it as it is and gently pull the petals apart. As it opens, the center of the flower may be colored with food coloring, or put on the tips only.)

   Used as a lotus, the flower should always have its head lifted and be very upright. Cut your lotus pad leaves from spinach leaves.

Showy Chrysanthemum

1 Peel a large, young carrot.

2 With your vegetable peeler or slicer, make many slices—all long and very thin. You are slicing the carrot in the upright position as it grows. When you have a dozen such cuts, divide into three lengths: short, medium, and long.

3 Take each slice and round both ends.

4 Place on chopping board and carefully fringe both ends by cutting many fine strips. Leave about 1″ at the center of each slice *uncut.*

5 Put these rounded, fringed strips into ice water and let them curl. This can be done a day ahead.

To assemble the flower, start with two of the long-fringed strips. Put one strip at right angle to the other. Add two of the medium strips on top of the longer slices, filling in the open areas. Finish with two of the shortest slices on top. Insert a bamboo skewer from the bottom (large) to the top (small). Use a circle cut from a grapefruit peel for center.

To use as an appetizer, make the flower as directed, but use shorter sliced lengths. For the center use:

Large, stuffed, green or black olive
Monterey Jack cheese
Pitted prune filled with cream cheese
Small, red cherry tomato
Pickled mushroom

Making Designs with Leek Leaves

The broad leek leaves or stalk are excellent for decorating a ham or fish on which a design or scene is to be used to enhance appearance. Select leeks with good green tops. Cut off the white onion-like segment.

1 To use the tubular leek stalk, blanch it in boiling water, in and out again fast.

2 Put under cold tap water to retain color.

3 With knife tip, open up the shaft of the stalk and split the tube in half. You will use both of these pieces in working with a design.

4 Cut the half-stalk into the length and shape you desire. Place it in the design planned against the surface with shiny green side facing outward. When using this against a salmon, first carefully remove the skin of the fish, and then place the design within the frame.

5 After placing the design, glaze with a light clear gelatin (to one package of gelatin, use one-half cup of water). Let it "set" to a brushing consistency and put over the design. If the gelatin gets too thick or tacky, add more hot water and stir.

Flower Cut

So simple to do, yet just one flower sparks up a dish. Try serving a dish of string beans or peas with just one carrot flower sitting on top. Comments are compliments! This cut, too, can be served either cooked or raw.

1 Use a 2″ piece of a vegetable that is symmetrical in shape.

2 Holding your knife at an angle, cut and remove a V shape around this piece. Cut into the piece about ½″ at an angle.

3 Turn the vegetable around and make a second cut of the V. Remove.

4 Repeat steps 2 and 3 for the number of petals you want. (A dogwood has 4; a daffodil has 5; etc.)

5 Now slice this notched piece into the thickness you desire and you have the outline of a flower petal.

6 Time permitting, you may further shape by rounding the petals, even cutting them more deeply in the center.

7 Develop a new hybrid.

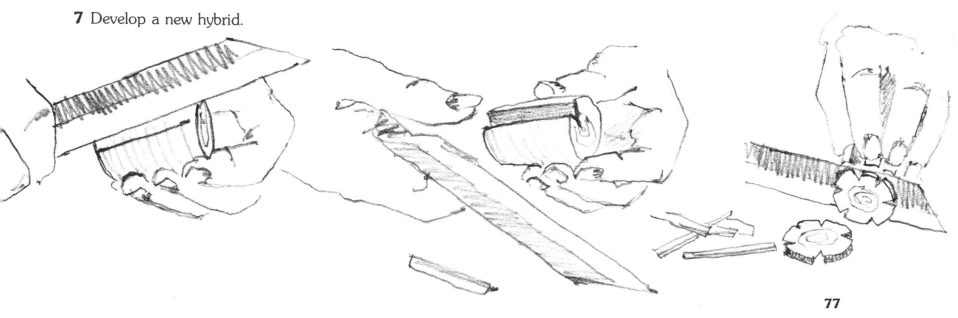

Centers for these flowers are made of a contrasting color. A hollowed disk, with or without fluted edge, made from a carrot, does nicely as a center for a turnip daffodil. Black olives, green and red pepper rounds, cheese, anchovies, all are possible centers. When using this cut in a flower arrangement, it is best to insert the pointed end of the bamboo skewer at a angle into the flower.

A daffodil is made from a turnip, with carrot chalice. The leaves of a green onion are made pointed before inserting the bamboo skewer through its center.

Flower Cut Stylized

Firm vegetables are necessary. This is another way of making similar flowers and is suited for those vegetables that do not grow symmetrical in shape.

1 Follow the diagram form for cutting.

2 Slice and continue to shape.

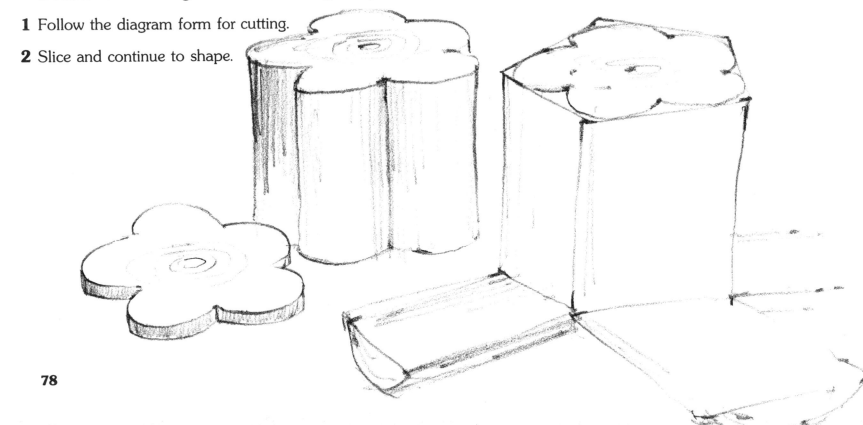

". . . one eats one's sandwich and an apple?"

An array of sandwiches showing various cuts in use. The very colorful antherium are made from red peppers with carrot stamin. The fan cut is used on pickles of okra. The celery twist as well as twisted orange, the broom cut of celery— each adds a finishing touch to the sandwich.

Antherium cut described on page 44; Celery twist described on page 55; Okra fan described on page 58.

Leek Flowers.

These flaring flowers add a festive note so complementary to many foods.
Cut is found on page 83.

Leek or Green Onion Flowers

Select vegetables with good tops.

1 Use a 2″ cut of leek.

2 Hold the leek firmly with the left hand and with your knife start about 1″ from the top, cutting lengthwise completely through the leek from top to bottom.

3 Make as many such cuts as the size of the leek can accommodate.

4 *Turn* the leek and again hold firmly.

5 Slice the uncut side from top to bottom and repeat steps 2 and 3.

6 Put the cut flower into a bowl of ice water for about half an hour until the strips flare.

7 In the center of the flare, add a bit of contrasting color: a stuffed olive, pimiento round, carrot strip, or orange peel.

N Cuts

This garnish can be used with soups, dessert, or main course, and the medium used is as varied as its use. It is most effective as the final touch as it can be done ahead of time.

1 Cut a strip from whatever medium you desire (orange, lemon, pimiento, pepper, celery, cooked whipped egg, cold meat, etc.) This strip can vary in size and width, approximately 1″ × ½″.

2 With knife tip make the strip into the figure N (see diagram).

3 As you open the N (pull apart) bring the right outer edge back *under* the center strip and over the remaining strip. *Easy!*

Butterfly Cut

This cut is a combination of two cuts: the simple circle cut and the N cut. Carrots are most often used as they are so colorful, but turnip and *daikon* can be made into larger butterflies. The cuts are fast and easy. However, in placing in ice water, allow sufficient water so the cuts are covered.

1 Peel the carrot.

2 Make one cut almost through the carrot.

3 Make another cut completely through the carrot.

4 Take this two-in-one-cut slice, which will be no thicker than ⅛″, and on the uncut portion of the slice make the N cut.

5 Place in ice water for the wings to spread. This spreading takes about an hour to do the cut justice. Perch the opened butterfly on a cooked vegetable of contrasting color.

Wedge Cuts

This cut is used mainly with fruit where the skin is left on and becomes a part of the color contrast.

1 Using a bright red apple, cut the apple into quarters.

2 With the skin side up, cut out triangle wedges, following the line of the quarter-wedge. Make at least two such cuts (see diagram).

3 By turning the apple, it is simple to keep the cuts precise.

4 Stack the cuts so that some of the white apple shows.

BUNNY WEDGE

Apple Bird

This is a fun undertaking. The wings of the bird are the wedge cuts stacked to give the impression of feathers moving.

1 Using the whole apple, make the base of the bird level. Put this base cut aside as it will be used for the head.

2 Cut the apple in half. Using only the top half of the apple, cut the upper portion in half.

3 Make the wedge cut in these two sections (forming wings), and lay these "wings" on the bottom part of the apple.

4 Shape the piece removed from the base to form a head and attach to the apple with a bamboo skewer piece.

Tomato Wedge

A tomato wedge is dramatic. As the fruit is soft, use a firm tomato.

1 Cut a piece from the tomato so it will lie squarely.

2 Cut from right to center at an angle to form first wedge cut.

3 Cut from left to center at same angle and complete wedge.

4 Remove wedge piece and repeat steps 2 and 3 in this wedged piece. The first wedge will be heavier than the remaining cuts.

5 Make as many wedges as the tomato will hold. Restack so the cut underneath the fruit will show. Place on your meat platter.

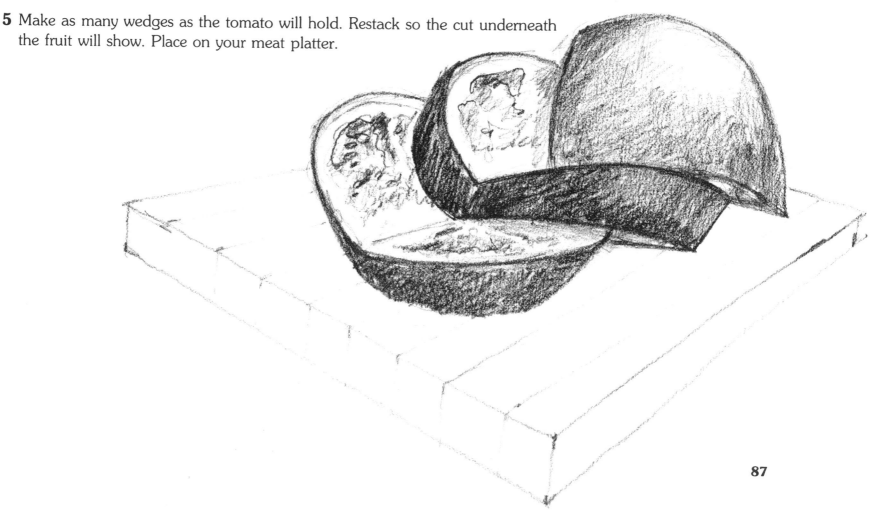

Fish Net Cut

Select a large, firm *daikon*.

1 Cut a piece from the *daikon* 2″ to 3″ long.

2 Make the sides straight, forming a rectangle. You will be using a continuous (bark) peel. The purpose of squaring off the vegetable is that it gives you a better guideline for the steps in making the net.

3 Insert a chopstick all the way through—dead center.

4 Cut one side (top) to center (chopstick), repeating this cut in equal portions the length of the piece, about ½″ apart.

5 Turn the *daikon* over (bottom) and repeat step 4. *Line each cut with its mate on the top side.* Cut to chopstick. Top and bottom cuts are equal distances apart.

6 Turn the *daikon* so the uncut side is now on top.

7 Place your knife so these next cuts lie in between the cuts just completed. Make the new cuts equal distances apart.

8 Turn the *daikon* over and cut the last remaining side, *lining this side with the cut you have just completed.* Remove the chopstick.

9 Start continuous peel. Work carefully for a uniform thickness. Work over the chopping block.

10 Stop when you have peeled close to the center. Be careful to avoid tearing. Listen! The *daikon* "talks" to you when you work close to the center. Rewind.

11 Salt the *daikon* heavily. Let it stand about 10 minutes as it "bleeds" and softens.

12 Place the cut, salted rectangle in a paper towel and squeeze out the excess moisture.

13 Unroll and arrange the diamond-shaped net.

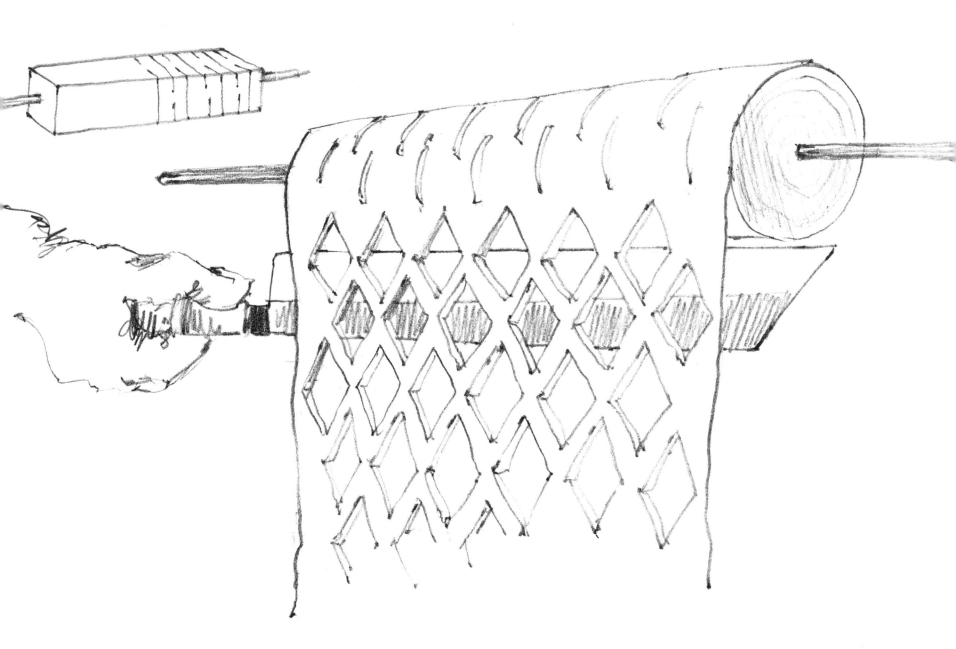

Cuts for Cucumber

In selecting a cucumber, use only the youngest ones and if possible those that have not been waxed. The English or Japanese style (long and thin) are recommended.

1 Cut a piece between 2″ and 3″ long.

2 Starting from the top end, slice thinly to ½″ from the bottom. Do not cut through base.

3 Let the outside slice remain straight. Bend the next slice back on itself (see diagram).

4 Repeat this step 3 or go back to step 2. The number of thin slice pieces within the cucumber suggests the pattern.

(*Note:* If cucumber is too crisp to bend back on itself, lightly salt the cucumber and let stand for a few minutes.)

Stand-up Cucumber

Follow the diagram for slicing.

1 Cut off a piece of cucumber, approximately 3″ long.

2 Midway in the cucumber, run your paring knife through the meat and leave the knife in while you angle cut.

3 Angle cut to the knife (see diagram).

Cucumber Rosettes

Select a medium-sized cucumber.

1 Peel cucumber lightly.

2 Using a slicer, cut as many long, thin slices as possible. Hold the cucumber in an upright position. (The slices must be thin.)

3 Discard the center with the heavy seeds.

4 Take one of the slices and fold it in half the long way of the slice. Place the folded piece on the chopping board and with knife tip cut many fine slits at an angle through the fold. This angle cut is only partially through the folded slice.

5 Take a large, stuffed green olive. Wrap the folded cut slice (cup edges up) around the olive. The folded edge *opens* as it is wrapped. Hold together with a toothpick or pack tightly in small square pan. Refrigerate until serving time.

Serve around a meat platter, or use as an appetizer.

(*Note:* A cherry tomato, red radish, cheese, or a ripe olive can be substituted for the olive.)

Tomato Mushrooms

Select firm, bright red cherry tomatoes or small salad tomatoes.

1 When using a cherry tomato, cut it in half. Set aside the blossom end half for use later.

2 Gently scoop out the meat from the remaining half. This half will form the tomato cap. Complete as many of these as you need.

3 Form a stem* for the mushroom cap from a turnip, jicama, or sunchoke, whichever is available. Make the stems larger at the bottom than at the top. A broad base is desired for easy standing. Start with a 2″ stem and cut to desired height.

4 Place the tomato cap on the white stem. Adjust the height and tilt. Place a skewer point or sharp toothpick through the tomato into the stem.

5 Put tiny dots of mayonnaise on the mushroom top.

   * An apple corer can be used for the stem section. This will give you a uniform, rather than tapered, stem. Make the base level.

Tomato Roses

A cherry tomato rose is very simple to do. Two different size cherry tomatoes are used. Be sure the fruit is firm and select tomatoes without blemishes.

1 Cut the small cherry tomato into four equal parts.

2 Scoop out the fruit with a spoon, leaving a shell.

3 Take the somewhat larger cherry tomato and repeat steps 1 and 2.

4 Now place the small cherry tomato within the larger tomato so that the petals lie in alternate layers.

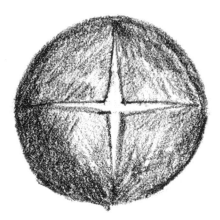

Tomato Peel Rose

This uses a solid ripe tomato without blemish.

1 Starting at stem end, cut the skin from the tomato in a thin, continuous spiral strip ½″ to ¾″ wide. This is your bark cut. Let the spiral rest on the cutting board until the entire tomato is peeled.

2 The final cut at the base is done in a solid piece.

3 Form the rose by wrapping the peel around the last solid piece removed from the tomato. Hold the thumb firmly in the center and form the flower around it.

4 Place either side up—whichever makes the shape you desire.

5 For a very tight rose, hold together with a bamboo skewer.

6 Use a circle of lemon peel for center.

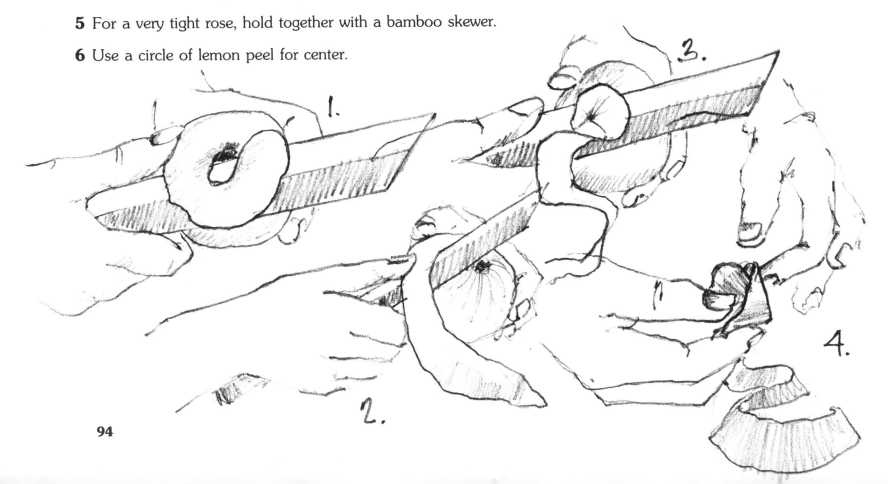

Tomato Rose

1 With the tip of your knife, equally divide a solid red tomato into eight equal parts. Start your cut at the base end of the tomato and do not let the knife cut more than ¼″ deep. This divisional cut will be to within ½″ from stem end.

2 Use your skewer as a guideline if you are not confident.

3 Gently lift up one of the petals at its tip and cleanly peel-cut this wedge-shaped piece to its base.

4 Repeat step 3 for the remaining petals.

5 Lay the petal cuts away from the exposed tomato.

Vegetable Rose

Tomatoes can be used here also, but this cut works exceptionally well with turnips, potatoes, beets, rutabagas, and the versatile *daikon*.

1 Peel the vegetable and make the vegetable as round as possible.

2 Cut off the stem end so vegetable sits erect.

3 Round edge of top by peeling.

4 Cut five petals around the bottom third of the vegetable. Use the tip of knife. Do not cut through the base.

5 Remove a very thin portion between the petals and the inner section by peeling with knife tip.

6 Cut five more petals in the rounded inner section. Stagger petals, being careful not to cut through base.

7 Repeat step 5.

8 Repeat step 6 procedure until center is reached.

9 Place point of knife in center of vegetable and twist carefully to open, or hollow out center, leave in shape of cup, and dice center with very fine slices.

10 Add food coloring and let stand (*daikon,* turnip, or rutabaga).

Rose with Petals

This rose can be fashioned from a carrot, *daikon,* or red beet. The *daikon* is a favorite as the thin petals take on food coloring beautifully.

1 Cut a *daikon* into three pieces, small, medium, and large (large piece is about 1-½″ long).

2 The bark cut is used—carefully cut around and around making the peel the same thickness. Work for a see-through thickness.

3 Lay the cut strip on the chopping block and cut individual petals in the shape of a rose petal. (Are you aware of how very different in shape is the rose petal from the camellia petal which is approached in the same way?)

4 Drop these petals into a bowl holding ice water.

5 Each petal is then cut a portion of the way at its base. This cut, at the base, is about one-fourth of the length of the petal, so that the base stem can be overlapped.

6 With an arm motion, start curving the petals by actually pulling the knife blade from the center outward to the tip. Repeat this several times until the petal has a full curve.

7 Return the petal to the ice water.

8 Complete each petal in this manner. There should be a minimum of eleven petals in all for a full rose. The rolling motion of the knife is always started at the center.

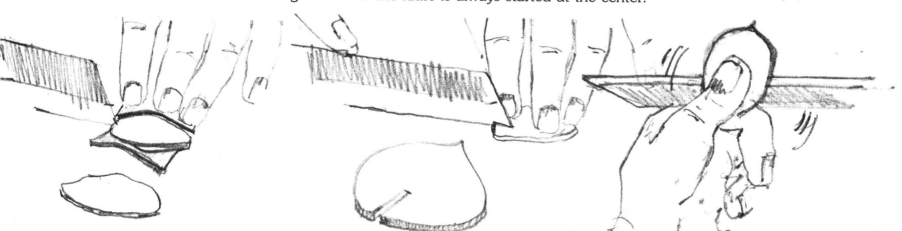

To Assemble the Rose

1 Cut a base for the rose 2″ long, using the *daikon*.

2 Dice cut the center to a depth of ¼″.

3 The outer edge is gently rounded.

4 Divide the center into slits about ¼″ deep to hold three curving petals (see diagram).

5 Lay the three smallest petals into the slits so their curl is over the center dice.

6 Using a ⅝″ brad, cross and pin together a medium-sized petal, facing the curled side toward the center of the rose. Fasten this piece *straight into* base.

7 Repeat step 6 going around the base completely.

8 Repeat steps 6 and 7 until all petals are attached to the 2″ base piece. If you wish the flower to be more open, reverse the petals so the curled edge faces downward. You have control of the flower size.

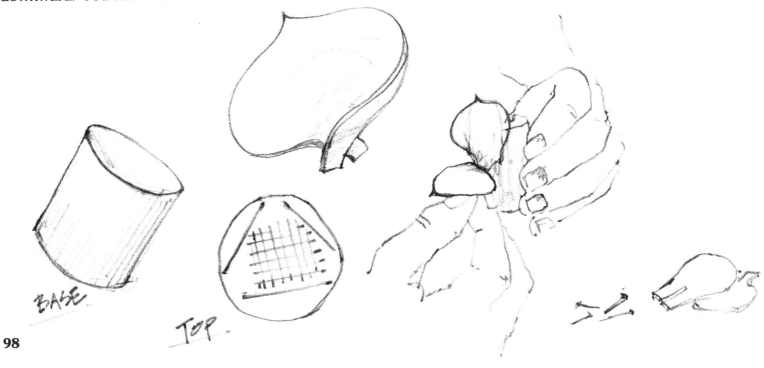

BASE

TOP

"When spring unlocks the flowers to paint the laughing soil."

The basket base is created from a Pamelo "the grapefruit-orange fruit." Radishes
in a variety of cuts emphasize the eye appeal. Carrot flowers using the pencil cut
are softened by the green onion whirls. Turnips found their space.
The black olive is a pleasing accent.

This modified cut is on page 67. Carrot flowers and turnips on page 54; Green onion whirls on page 83.

The shrimp boat's a-coming!

Zucchini, parboiled, has a different usage as a scooped out container for delicate shrimp. The lemon wedge serves as a flag. The grated *daikon* adds a taste treat.

Cut on page 69.

102

Camellia

The *daikon* is used for making this flower. Know the difference in petal shape and cut each individual petal in the same manner as the rose. The base of the petal has the short cut for the overlap. The curl is formed by starting at center and working out for a fringe curl. The base of the camellia is more triangular in shape and 1-½″ tall.

1 Gently scoop out center, leaving a slightly raised portion in the middle (see diagram).

2 Assemble the petals—small, medium, large—by overlapping the base of each petal and pinning the brad *straight into* the triangular base.

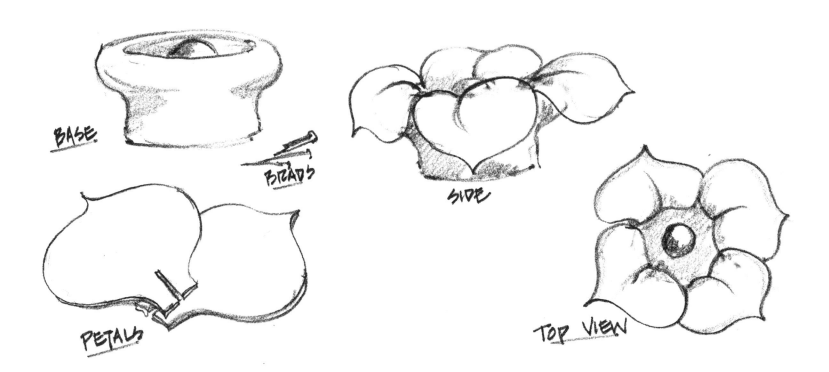

BASE

BRADS

SIDE

PETALS

TOP VIEW

Chrysanthemum

This is made and assembled in the same manner only the petals are shaped and each petal is divided into thirds. The flare of the curl is more pronounced as the petal is divided.

1 A carrot base is suggested here as it is firmer and more petals are necessary for making this flower. The base is 2″ tall. Sometimes you can find a carrot with a clean green top that can be used effectively.

2 Bark cut a number of petals, small, medium, and large. These petals are pointed in shape.

3 Cut each petal into thirds, making each tip pointed, and then start flaring the petals as you do for the petal rose.

4 As a chrysanthemum is flatter in shape than the rose or camellia, you will be pinning more large petals into the base than small ones.

5 Perhaps you will be able to try the spider chrysanthemum, making many fine cuts for each petal before curling. Curl sharply, then let the ice water work for you.

(*Note:* In curling petals another system is employed by using the palm of the hand. The petal is placed in the palm. The heel of the knife handle is pressed into the palm in a circular motion. This type of curl does not have the fringed edge but is satisfactory for very large petals.)

Peony/Zinnia

A carrot with its color variations is welcome for this formal flower.

1 Cut your petals in small, medium, and large sizes.

2 Use the bark cut and peel evenly around each piece. The bark peel is in the cupped shape of the petal.

3 Form a tip for each peel, shaping the petal as a half finger.

4 Shape the three sizes of petals and place in holding ice water.

5 The base of the flower is from a carrot that is tapered from the bottom to the top. The base is about 2″ tall.

6 Fasten five of the smaller petals around the top with a bamboo skewer broken into small pieces.

7 Alternate the petals of the second row and repeat for each additional row until the flower is complete. The largest petals are the last to be fastened to the base.

(*Note:* The bamboo skewers are easier to keep in place than the metal brads.)

Carrot Trees

French carrots or the coreless carrots are an ideal size.

1 After peeling, thin slice the carrot from the stem end to the root end.

2 If uniform in size, stack three of the pieces together and make notches on either side forming tree limbs.

3 Arrange on plate so the edges show.

(*Note:* Wings for a bird are made the same way, only one side is notched.)

Stupid hot melons
Rolling
Like fat idiots
Out from leafy shade!

BASHO

Picking vegetables for their shape will become second-nature to you as you grow in this art. The field of melons opens new vistas.

Turkey Melon

1 Select a fairly large watermelon or a crenshaw. Cut a thin slice from the stem end of the melon. This will be for the base. Make certain the melon will stand upright.

2 Determine the size of the body (how much you want to fill with various seasonal fruits). Put in a long bamboo skewer as your guide line.

3 Start to remove the upper portion of the melon, cutting down to the skewer, which helps to keep the melon from splitting. Work from the outside toward the center (neck).

4 Work slowly. Visualize, as you remove parts of the melon, the neck of the turkey. Gradually taper the sides of the neck. Headless, crazy looking bird!

5 Remove the fruit adhering to the neck the last.

6 Using a short skewer (cut to desired length) put on an apple or orange head. The head sits astride the top of the neck cut.

7 Make a beak from the discarded rind. Add eyes if you wish. Add a small bunch of grapes below the beak. Hold in place with short skewers.

8 Fill the body cavity with fruit.

9 Using short, medium, and long skewers, fashion a fan-tail for the turkey. These skewers, filled with colored fruit balls, stand along the outer-back edge of the cavity. Alternate different colored melon balls on the skewer.

A Whale-of-a Cut

1 Select a watermelon that is long. Use the larger portion of the melon for the head. cut a thin slice off of base so the melon will not roll.

2 Determine the depth of cavity you want to fill with fruit. Put your skewer in the middle at that point.

3 Approximately one-fourth of the distance from the head-end to the skewer start a slice. It is well to place another skewer at this point the same depth as the first. Melons tend to crack. Work slowly. Do not try to force or remove too large a piece.

4 Remove the melon from the outer skewer to the middle skewer. Set fruit aside.

5 The back half of the melon has not been touched. Take your pencil and draw on the rind an outline of a flipping tail. Cut a paper pattern if you feel it is necessary. Start to remove this portion of melon and rind.

6 Gradually remove the meat from the tail. Set aside.

7 Scoop out the cavity.

8 With knife tip create a face for your whale—winking, cross-eyed, smiling. Put in the mouth.

9 The green onion cut (the leek or green onion cut) using a fairly long shaft can be placed in the spouting area! Your whale is now ready to be filled.

Melon Rose

Select a ripe melon. Cut the melon into thirds. Place one end of the cut melon on your chopping block and remove the rind. Remove the rind in large segments as some of these pieces will be formed into leaves.

1 Start at the top to fashion small petals. Make your petals irregular. The petals should be small at the top or center and gradually increase in size as you work down the melon.

2 Vary the depth of the cuts. Use the tip of your blade. At an angle, cut into the outlined petal cut and remove the slivers of meat.

3 Vary the size of the petals.

4 When the flower has been completely formed and the slivers of meat removed, using knife tip, remove the bottom edge. This gives a softer line effect—not a straight edge—for placing on a serving plate.

5 Arrange on a platter. Make large rose leaves from spinach or fashion leaves from the green melon rind.

Serve with a fruit knife and let guests slice their own.

Melon Sunflower

Select a firm ripe melon. Standing the melon on the stem end, determine the half-way point between the ends, and cut. This will give you two half melons to work with and for serving. Remove the seeds. Peel.

1 Placing the cut side down on your chopping block, outline a circle with a round cookie cutter.

2 Using knife tip, angle cut into the circle's edge and remove that portion of meat. This angle cut emphasizes the center circle.

3 Lightly cut many fine slits across the center circle from side to side. Turn the melon and make fine slits in the opposite direction.

4 Starting below the finished circle, outline a petal. Use your knife again at an angle and remove the meat along the outside edge of petal. Work around the melon, making petals of uniform size.

5 When the first row of petals is completed, alternate cutting a second row. Alternate each new row of petals.

6 Texture is added to the sunflower by removing a thin elongated slice from the middle of each petal.

7 For serving, cut spinach leaves are placed around the single large flower.

   (*Note:* Persian melons work well here, too.)

A Final Thought

Remember that the mind is the birthplace of the future. So, as your fingers become more agile and your imagination more fertile, you will discover that there are many more ways to enhance the color scheme for serving food. Create your own egg penquin with ripe olives; make your lemon pig with curly celery tail; let your relish tray be decorative as well as edible. Entertaining becomes fun. Follow the simple rule that a good Japanese restaurant adheres to:

never let a cup be empty, never let it be too full,
the guest must be put in a good mood, made to feel on the brink of paradise.

Your knife and you can project this special feeling through the final touch.

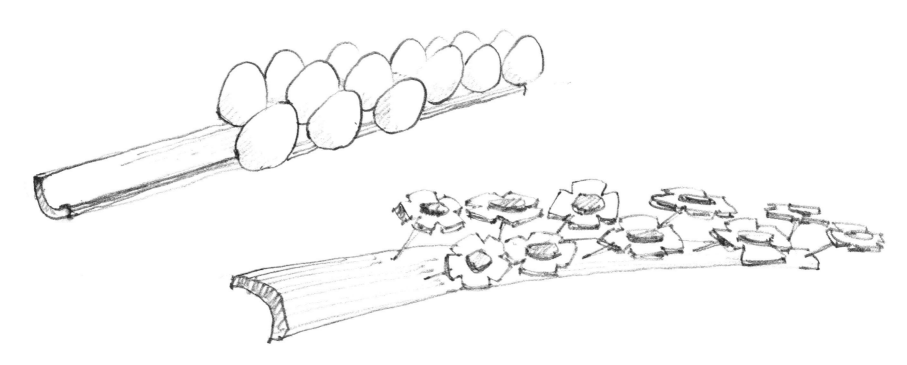

THE FINAL
TOUCH
APPLIED

You take a scarlet pepper-pod, apply
Two wings of gauze, and look—a dragonfly!

BASHO

Have you ever sat beside someone humped over his plate, slurping, stuffing food into his mouth, with conversation limited to a grunt? Did you have the urge to say: "Hey! Sit up! Look around you! Eating is a time to leave your stresses behind you. It is a time to thoroughly relax and enjoy. It is a time of laughter and sharing."

A set time for meals has almost become obsolete since family life-styles have changed. This restructuring started to gain momentum in the early seventies. Being punctual for meals is no longer an ingredient in family life. Changed, too, is the family sit-down-to-the-table. Many families exist without ever seeing each other. Being able to use a knife and fork properly is no longer socially imperative. Conversation, table manners, and good eating habits all have been pushed aside by this changed restructuring of living routine.

The role of the parent has seen the greatest disruption. The head of the house has had his authority usurped. The role of the mother is likely to be one of breadwinner. What has this to do with food? Eating habits are now guided by a new master—television. Television has brought an overall awareness to exotic dining, luxurious resort living, sporty cars, dark glasses, blue-jean smartness, and the paramount need for two breadwinners within the family circle. Why? The good things of life have become geared to *now*. All things must be enjoyed *now*. The child must have better than the parent.

This mass deemphasis on time for meals has insidiously pursued the trend of changing values. Self-analysis and "doing your own thing" are healthy attitudes as long as the individual is in control and recognizes a goal. Responsibility in all age groups lies heavily with each individual. "You eat what *you* want to become" (Japanese concept). *Food* and *you* are one in the act of becoming. You advertise to the world and friends the opinion you hold of yourself. You announce publicly your ability to cope with your life-style. Nutrition is the gambit.

Nutrition, well-balanced meals, and health foods all conjure strange images of their advocates. They are shunned probably because each demands discipline and sacrificing the frostings of easy living. Food has been recognized as a crutch in handling stress. The ever present challenge is to prepare foods so each family member seeks the healthful route over the easier, more expensive junk food. Natural food exponents have conscientiously forced upon our menus and placed in our health food and super markets foods that are fibrous and bulky. The training has begun. Taste what you eat. Learn some of the simplest cuts for food so you can make the commonest garden vegetable a part of savoir-vivre!

We are back to where we started—knife skill—knife skill that a child can perform, that entices the imagination, that shows that you *care,* and that *saves* time and dollars! Who would want to prepare a meal without it?

Browsing mid the mushrooms.

The *Ainu* carved bear adds interest to the simple flower cuts of mushrooms and crocus made of radish.

Cut on page 71.

120

". . . and then my heart with pleasure fills and dances with the daffodils."

Even the eggplant has an interesting shape for bases. The petaled flowers are made from turnip and rutabaga with carrot centers and green onion leaves.

Cut on page 77.

ORCHESTRATION

Time now to share some recipes that lend themselves to the suggested knife cuts and appear fantastic. These recipes are all easy to do.

Realize that the moment you present a single unusual cut for everyday fare you are showing love and pride in what you serve. You are a caring person—not careless of the little things that enrich life.

Young and old alike will tune in to beauty in food preparation. Know the history, beliefs, facts, and stories about vegetables. Share! I pass this *"on"* to you.

Asparagus

This stalky plant is believed to be native of the Mediterranean and Asia Minor. In ancient days the Greeks and Romans preferred its flavor in the wild state. In his writing of 200 B.C., Cato gave explicit instructions for its culture.

Europeans prefer the white, large asparagus to the green. In Europe it is served to be eaten with the fingers. Asparagus places itself in the epicurean class as it lends itself well to so many types of sauces. Whether steamed, boiled, or stir-fried, the stalk should be tender but *firm*. When using large stalks, peel the stalk below the tip. You will find that you can use more of the vegetable this way, and the stalk underneath the peel is tender. Asparagus contains alkaloids which help to break up uric acid within the human body.

Soya Asparagus

Wash, clean, and peel 1 lb. of asparagus. Cut pieces about 1-½" long. Use roll cut *(rangiri)*. Heat wok or fry pan and oil the surface of pan with an oiled paper towel. When the pan is hot, toss in the heavier end pieces, leaving tips to the last. Stir fry about 3 minutes. Add 1 tablespoon soya sauce. Continue to stir-fry until liquid is absorbed into the cut ends turning them a golden brown. Serve hot.

Beans

This vegetable, grown all over the world, has many varieties. It is quite easily grown in the garden, but apparently each country in which it is grown cultivates its own special type of bean. In the Greek and Roman culture, beans were used as ballots. In casting a vote the white bean was "yes" and the black bean was "no."

Beets

As early as 830 A.D. beets were planted by the monks of the Benedictine monastery in Switzerland. Charlemagne meticulously kept a record of vegetables grown in his garden and beets were among those listed.

Belgian Endive

This sprout is fairly new to the United States. As people have traveled more extensively, its popularity has gained but it is exorbitant in price. The endive is imported from Belgium where it has been used as an additive to coffee. The French also use it this way. The sprout is a member of the chicory family. Shaped like a small ear of corn, its color is creamy white with pale green tips. The leaves are tight. Belgian endive is loved for its lack of calories. It can be eaten raw in salads or is excellent when steamed. Try baking it whole in chicken stock and a bit of lemon juice.

Belgian Endive and Garden Beet Salad

Boil tender young beets. Skin when cooled and cut *(sengiri)* into strips. Place these strips in a separate container. Chill.

Cut the Belgian endive into strips, also, matching the same length as the beets. One endive will serve two people. Keep in a separate container. Chill.

When ready to serve, use romaine lettuce cut into bite-sized pieces for the salad base. Toss each vegetable separately in your favorite French dressing to which you have added a scant teaspoon of dry mustard. Place the two vegetables side by side on the romaine base. The contrast is vivid.

Bok Choy

This oriental vegetable is shaped like celery only it is loose-leafed. The leaves are very dark on a pure white stalk. Both the leaves and stalk are used in cooking. *Bok choy* is a good source of vitamin A. The leaves take seconds to wilt, whereas, the white stalks take longer. The heart of this plant may be used like celery in salads. The leaves adapt themselves to scissor cutting when a special design is needed.

Bok Choy with Pork, Chicken, or Beef

Slice pork, using *ranami-giri* (diagnonal cut). Marinate the meat in

1 T cornstarch
1 T soya sauce
1 T *mirin* wine

Reserve bone to make *dashi* (soup stock).
Cut the washed *bok choy* in diagonal slices and stir fry. Put the heavier white stalk in the wok first and when almost tender add the grean leafy part.

Add ½ cup of pork *dashi* (soup stock). Cover and steam cook for a minute. Stir-fry the pork slices in skillet. This may be done first and set aside (after it has marinated) then added to the *bok choy* just before serving. More cornstarch may be added if necessary.

Broccoli

This vegetable, known in Europe for 2000 years, became a success story of the 1920s in America. Broccoli appears in the market the year around. The California broccoli growers of the San Jose valley raised fields of the lush green vegetable which had no outside market. At a meeting the Italian growers decided to gamble and ship a refrigerated car to Boston. Broccoli became an instant success. The annual consumption today is 151 million pounds and this figure is due to be increased as broccoli is appearing more and more on relish trays and eaten uncooked.

The Italian word "brocco" means an arm or branch. The broccoli plant is made up of many such arms. It is related to the cauliflower family. The Romans cultivated broccoli in the first century B.C.

In buying broccoli, pick stalks that are tightly closed and of a deep green color. This vegetable is rich in calcium and iron, and it contains riboflavin. It is excellent when steamed. When steaming this vegetable, douse it in cold water immediately when it is fork-tender to retain its color brilliance. The trunk of the broccoli, like thick asparagus stalks, is more tender when peeled and then sliced.

Broccoli and Beef

Wash 1 lb. of broccoli and peel the thick stem. Use the *sengiri* (strip) cut, following the pattern suggested by the green flowers.

Cut ½ lb. of beef into thin strips. Brown the beef slowly in 1 T oil and 1 garlic clove.

When beef strips are cooking, add the broccoli and 1 T soya sauce, ½ cup water. Toss gently together and let the beef and broccoli simmer.

Carrot

The cartoon character of Bugs Bunny with his passion for carrots is an example of what can happen to a vegetable to become popular with children. This common garden vegetable is grown the world over. It is popular in every language. Seeds dating 2000 B.C. were found in the lake dwellings of central Switzerland. It was used as a cure for stomach aches in Roman days.

The carrot is a member of the parsley family. The top of the wild carrot looks like Queen Anne's lace. In the United States the long variety of carrot is more readily available than the popular short carrot found in Europe. In Germany the carrot is made into a type of coffee. In selecting carrots, choose the crisp, bright orange carrot. The more orange the color, the higher the natural sugar content.

Marinated Carrots

Peel 2 pounds carrots. Using the roll cut make each piece about 1″ to 1-½″ in length. Place in boiling salted water and cook until barely tender. Drain well.

Make marinade:

1 can tomato soup	**1 tsp. dry mustard**
¼ cup honey	**¼ tsp. cayenne pepper**
½ cup oil	**1 clove of garlic, crushed**
¾ cup cider vinegar	**Tabasco, to taste**

Cook until well blended.

Slice:

1 large salad onion into thin rings
1 bell pepper into 3″ strips

Combine the cooked carrots and sliced vegetables. Pour the hot marinade over and refrigerate for 24 hours.

Cauliflower

Cauliflower is a member of the cabbage family. It grows best in cool and damp climates. The outer dark green leaves protect the head from the sun, actually blanching the head.

Celery

Celery is a member of the parsley family. It is made up mostly of water and adds bulk to the diet. In the 1600s the whiter celery stalk was considered the most desirable. Tastes have changed and now the bright fresh green has taken precedence. The French have promoted the use of the entire plant, especially the leaves, which they dry and use in soups. In buying celery, select a plant with a big shank, glossy and firm.

The ancient Romans used the celery stalk as a blood purifier. Many of the writings of that time refer to celery as a stimulant and tonic. A cupful of celery contains about 9 calories.

Chayote

The color is as exquisite as jade! This vegetable, new to the supermarket, is imported from Mexico. The name sounds mysterious. In Mexico the entire plant is used. The very young shoots are eaten like asparagus. The tuberous roots are similar to potatoes. The stalk of the plant is woven into hats and baskets. This tropical plant is known by many names depending on where grown. It is a squash. In shape, the chayote is round or pear-shaped and about 6″ long. It appears to have closed fingers. It contains a large seed which hardens as the plant grows older.

The chayote is light green in color. The unique quality is that after steaming it retains a vivid jade-green tone. The meat is fiberless, firm, but sweet. The calories are few. Used in contrast with meat, the vibrant green has eye appeal.

Steamed Chayote Fingers

Select a chayote that is about 6″ long and firm. Cut into finger strips about ½″ wide. Steam until tender. Serve with:

butter, salt, and pepper
a touch of nutmeg
a touch of ginger juice
lemon juice and salt

Chinese Cabbage

This celery-shaped cabbage plant comes from China. It is so delicate in flavor that it can be substituted for lettuce. The Chinese cabbage is available the year around. On the West Coast it is sometimes referred to as the Napa Valley cabbage.

The leaves of the Chinese cabbage are a yellow-green with a strong white center. The white center stalk can be shaped for antherium flowers and used as a centerpiece or a meat garnish. This vegetable is used extensively in all types of oriental cooking.

Cucumber

Cucumbers seem to fall into two classes: you like them or you don't. There is no happy in-between. One of the early lovers of cucumbers was Emperor Tiberius who ate cucumbers every day. In fact he was so fond of them he had a moveable frame constructed for their cultivation. This made it possible for him to have cucumbers wherever he went. The cucumber is one of the oldest known squashes, dating back almost 3000 years. It is alleged that Columbus had cucumbers planted in Haiti in 1494.

People have tagged the cucumber as a "distressing" food. Its burp and various methods employed for elimination of the burp is almost a story in itself. The Japanese claim that if a slice is removed from each end of the cucumber and the cut ends rubbed in the palm of the hand, the burp is destroyed as the juices start to form.

Cures and health secrets attributed to the cucumber range from applying the juice to clear skin disorders, to aid split nails because of its high potassium content, to promote the growth of hair due to silicon, to cure pyorrhea, and to resuscitate people from fainting spells. Cosmetologists have a wide selection of products on the shelves—all healthful. It is supposed to act as a body coolant in the summer. A single plant can yield from 25 to 125 cukes. The water content of a cucumber is high. They are best when crunchy fresh from the field and not too large.

Lazy Man's Stuffed Cucumber

Wash the cucumber. With your peeler remove a thin strip of the skin, alternating around the cucumber. Cut off the ends and then cut the cucumber in 2″ chunks. With apple corer remove the seeds.

Stuff the hollowed out cucumber with a well-mixed combination of:

3 oz. pkg. cream cheese with chive or pimiento cream cheese
(soften cheese with 1 T sour cream)
baby shrimp

Pack the hollowed cucumber tightly. Refrigerate. Cut in ½″ slices just before serving.

Daikon

It is believed this radish originated in China. It is a member of the rape family. In Chinese cooking it is sometimes referred to as a turnip because of its size. The Japanese considered it a radish—a "big root" white radish—not to be confused with our tiny red radish. Records reveal it was grown in Japan as early as the eighth century.

The *daikon* is as important to the Japanese economy as potatoes have been to the American. Over 34 varieties are harvested. It is popular dried as well as fresh. The "dried" *daikon* is usually in its natural color or dyed a vivid yellow. Dried it is called *takuwan*. The shredded *(sengiri)* can be purchased in cellophane bags. It is not an unusual sight to see the long white radish draped over a fence or hung from trees to dry. The radishes are sometimes formed into ladders and allowed to dry until about one-half to one-third their original size.

This vegetable contains high quantities of vitamin C and is credited with aiding digestion and other stomach ailments. It can be eaten raw, boiled, steamed, or pickled. As the radish becomes old, it becomes smelly and strong. Select a radish or a segment of a radish that is firm and has a glossy skin surface.

The *daikon* is so much a part of the daily life of the Japanese that the people have used the name in coined phrases. If you wish to be popular you do not refer to your girlfriend's legs as being *"daikon-ashi"*—radish-legs. The poor performance of an actor can be spoken of as a *daikon*-actor.

Daikon, Pork, Apples, and Lemon

This style of cooking several vegetables cut in different shapes, is referred to as *onishime.* This dish becomes most attractive with a sprig of parsley for each serving.

Cut a pork steak into cubes. Marinate in saki to cover.

Peel *daikon, wa-giri* style (round 1″ pieces). Roll each piece in flour and boil 1 minute in hot water. Drain.

Peel apples and cut apples into eighths. Place in salt water until ready to use.

Heat skillet and cook pork until evenly brown. Add the soup stock *(dashi)* made from the steak bone, about ½ cup. Cook 10 minutes.

Add the *daikon* and apples. Cook over medium heat. When fork-tender remove first the *daikon* then add to the pork and apples 1 T sugar and 1 T soya sauce. Cook until juice is gone.

Squeeze the juice of a lemon over the apple. Add more sugar to make a glaze. Cut from the lemon peel thin strips of lemon skin. Mix.

Jerusalem Artichoke

When is an artichoke *not* an artichoke? When it's a Jerusalem artichoke. The name is misleading. A Jerusalem artichoke is not an artichoke nor is it a member of the choke family. It is a bulb—a sunflower bulb grown in Italy and loved for its very large, showy flower. The Italian name, *girasole,* has been replaced by Jerusalem. This bulb comes in a variety of colors. The most familiar bulb in our markets is light brown in color and very thin skinned. It is sweet and crisp and is usually sold in plastic bags. This very knobby, potato-like bulb is sometimes called a sunchoke. When peeled, if the bulb is not quickly immersed in salt water, it will turn brown. The French are partial to this bulb. Champlain reported that the Indians grew the Jerusalem artichoke on Cape Cod in 1605.

The Jerusalem artichoke adapts itself well for carving of small birds. Use it also for fish and as a base for the tomato mushroom. It is high in water content and low in calories. The bulb is interchangeable in many recipes for water chestnuts. It is excellent as a crunchy appetizer. The bulb should be a favorite of diabetics as it contains the inulin enzyme.

Pickled Jerusalem Artichoke

Use sterilized pint jars. Pack the jars with the peeled artichokes. Use the stylized flower-shaped design and put the flower cut in the jar so the flower-face faces outward. These cuts should be about ½″ thick. This makes an attractive gift.

Mix:

1 sprig of fresh dill
1 large clove of peeled garlic
pinch of cayenne

Pour over and fill to top a brine which has boiled 5 minutes:

1 cup of cider vinegar
2 cups of water
2 T salt

Seal the jars and let stand for two weeks.

Jicama

Popularity of this root for snacks is increasing. This very large, light brown tuber is used in many ways in Mexico. It is a member of the morning glory family. The jicama weighs from 1 to 6 pounds. It is satisfactory for carving large showy flowers for a buffet. When immersed in food coloring, it takes well to the color. The jicama is respected by the Mexicans for the brilliant flowers that grow on this vine.

In selecting a jicama for serving, pick a firm root. These roots are like a four-leaf clover in shape. The outer brown skin of the root peels off like a tomato skin. The outer skin is quite stringy, so it is necessary to peel the root. The meat is very white and quite watery. It can be shaped into any number of simple cuts. The root itself can be carved into a dahlia flower.

Cold turkey.

The simple N cut of the red pepper is dramatic against the white meat of the turkey. Your roll cut (energy-saver) applied to the asparagus makes each piece become individual.

N cut described on page 84; Roll cut on page 53.

"And weave but nets to catch the wind."

A Dungeness crab is entangled in its *daikon* net.
Cut described on page 88.

Leek

Wales has distinguished the leek! It made the leek into a symbol of courage for the Welsh went into battle wearing not feathers in their caps but a *leek!* In this way the Welsh were able to identify themselves from the Saxons. The date of March 1 commemorates their victory.

This year-round vegetable, which is so subtle in its flavoring, is almost a luxury item. It is a member of the onion family and so mild that people who cannot tolerate onions can eat leek. It complements soups, salads, and stews. Nero ate leeks in oil to improve his voice.

The leek grows about 15″ tall. The root part of the leek is bleached white by covering with soil. The leaves are folded around the root and the plant must be carefully washed free of soil. In buying leeks, look for a stalk with leaves tightly rolled. Check to see if the stalk is woody. The entire stalk can be used in cooking. The French made the leek an essential ingredient of vichyssoise.

Carrot and Leek Casserole

In a buttered casserole, place:

3 cups of grated-coarsely carrot
1 cup of slivered leek tops.
1 T water
1 T margarine

Bake, covered, for one half hour at 325° oven. Just before serving, place in the center of the casserole a flower fashioned from the white bulb of the leek and thinly sliced, together with an angular cut leaf from the green stalk.

Okra

This hairy, finger-shaped pod with a sticky quality is sometimes named gumbo, depending on where it is grown. The okra found its way into Louisiana where it became popular in soups. The plant is native to Africa and little is known of its origin. Perhaps the African slaves brought it into this country. The vegetable is not popular in Europe. It is found in many dishes from the Middle East.

There are several varieties of okra. It takes well to freezing. The seeds are high in protein. The vegetable is always cooked. In purchasing the green pods, check to see if the outer surface is firm and free from blemish.

Fried Okra

Wash 1 lb. of young okra. Cut off stems and, using the diagonal cut, form pieces about ¼" thick. Par boil for 5 minutes in salted water. Drain.

Roll the okra in yellow cornmeal that has been seasoned with salt and pepper. Better results are gained if you will let the okra stand for 15 minutes before frying. Drain on paper towels and serve hot. Add a touch of garlic salt for interesting flavor.

Onion

A widely cultivated plant, the onion came to us from Asia. Inscribed on the Great Pyramid of Gizeh, built 5000 years ago, are the cost figures over a period of 20 years for the food of the slave builders—onions, radishes, and garlic. When the children of Israel fled Egypt they regretted having to leave the onion behind for they had grown accustomed to its uses.

Temples of the Greeks and Romans often included sculptures of the onion. They used the onion for medicine as well as food. It was prescribed as a cure for laryngitis, colds, fever, and poor eyesight. Warts were treated with onion juice. A bunch of onions hanging at the door entrance was supposed to keep the bad germs away from the house.

General Grant, believing onions could cure dysentery, refused to move his army until three wagonloads of onions were shipped to him. Onion poultices were applied for chest colds.

When peeling large quantities of onions, refrigerate them first. This helps to keep the tears from flowing.

Salad Onion Casserole

4 cups of diced sweet salad onion
½ cup Ronzoni Orzo 47 (macaroni)
2 T butter
½ cup shredded Swiss cheese
½ cup milk

Dice and saute the onions in 2 T butter. Set aside. Cook the Orzo 47 in boiling salted water for ten minutes. Drain. Combine and mix well all ingredients. Put in a greased casserole. Cover and bake for 1 hour in 300° oven.

To serve. Cut fresh red or green peppers into "N" design. Arrange on top and put under broiler for 1 minute.

Dramatic effect is created by parboiling a small onion which is then skinned and made into the chrysanthemum cut. Put this one flower as a decoration for the casserole. The chrysanthemum onion should be added during the last fifteen minutes of cooking. A rectangle of yellow cheese placed in the very center of the flower can be added at the last minute. Broil so the tips barely start browning.

Sesame

The name itself—sesame—conjures exotic images. The plant was first cultivated in Northern Africa and its oil was known in the Euphrates Valley as early as 1600 B.C. Sesame was mentioned in Egyptian writings of that era. The East Indies called it "thunderbolt" because they claimed sesame had powers to open secret hiding places. In India it is prized as a cooking oil. In India the seed is often referred to as benniseed. In Greece the plant was sacred to Hecate, the goddess of the underworld and of witchcraft. Many spells were dependent on its use.

In most recent years sesame has changed from being an ornament to foods and is now sold in bulk. The oil from the seeds is polyunsaturated and contains vitamin E. It is rich in calcium and in vitamin C. The seeds, a good source of protein, when ground taste and smell much like peanut butter. As an additive, the black sesame seeds are attractive.

To toast sesame seeds, place the seeds in a skillet on medium heat. The seeds turn a delicate shade of brown after you hear them pop three times. When browning large quantities of the seeds, use a cookie sheet, stir the seeds away from the sides, and watch to see that the color does not become too dark. For grinding the seeds, the *suribachi* (stringed bowl with wooden pestle) is easy to use.

Sesame Sauce

This sauce may be used with spinach, string beans, cauliflower, or asparagus. Make it up ahead of time.

Toast 2 T of sesame seeds to a light brown. Grind seeds to bring out fragrance. Add 2 T soya sauce and 1 T sugar or honey to the ground seeds. Mix.

HELPFUL HINTS

Spinach remains a bright green color when cooked in boiling salted water for a few minutes, blanched immediately under cold water, before returning to stove on off-heat.

String Beans and **Broccoli** are treated in like manner.

Cucumbers lose their burp when the ends are cut off, rubbed vigorously in the palm of the hand until the juice starts to flow. Remove the seeds and pulp. Slice paper thin crosswise. Sprinkle heavily with salt. Stand 10 minutes. Rinse with cold water and press out excess juice.

Onions are less likely to make you cry when sliced if the onion is held under cold running water or refrigerated before slicing.

Mushrooms are cleaned and whitened by putting 1 tbls. vinegar in a plastic bag with sufficient water to cover the mushrooms. Swish the mushrooms around in the bag. Repeat if they are very dirty. Rinse, clip stem, and the mushroom is ready for use.

Lettuce remains sweet when the core is removed. This can be easily accomplished by placing the lettuce core end down on your chopping block; pick up the lettuce and set it down *sharply* on its core. The core now twists out cleanly.

Asparagus takes less time to cook when it is roll cut.

Eggs, hard-boiled, will peel easily when cooked in water in which 1 tbls. vinegar has been added, and cooled quickly under cold tap water.

Meat, Fish, or **Fowl** will not stick to the broiling pan when broiler grill is first heated.

Shrimp cut with several small slits on the underside will not curl while cooking.

Carrots that are a bright orange in color are usually sweeter.

TOOLS OF THE ART

Knife skill demands a sharp knife—actually it is the only tool needed. Before rushing out to purchase an assortment of gadgets, discover what you can accomplish with the knife alone.

1. *Bowl with ice cubes and water.* A metal bowl is colder and the vegetables start to curl more quickly when they are shaped and then put into this type of container.

2. *A vegetable peeler.*

3. *Wooden or metal skewers.* These can be purchased in a number of lengths. Appetizers presented on skewers are easy to handle.

4. *Food coloring.* Food coloring can be used with a limited number of vegetables.

5. *Brads (measuring ½" to ⅝").* Brads are easier to use when forming a petaled rose. Brads have a tendency to rust, which can be prevented by adding oil to the container.

Most of these items are in your kitchen. A child's wood-working tool set can be purchased. The shape of these tools lets you work faster when performing some of the more complicated cuts. In the professional set purchased in Tokyo are the following items:

Left curved blade knife
Right curved blade knife
Half-crescent-shaped tool in four different sizes
V-shaped tool in four different sizes
Drill
Small pliers
3″ metal bar
Needlepoint tool

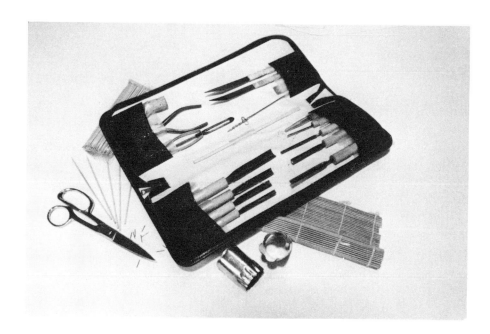

WHICH CUT TO USE FOR DINNER TONIGHT?

Asparagus   Cooked   Roll cut

Bean, Green or Wax Cooked   Roll cut
                                        French cut

Beet   Cooked   Dice
                                        Cut into shapes with cutter
                                        Strip or shred
                                        Slice
                       Uncooked   Cut rose petals
                                        Cut as rosette

Broccoli   Cooked   Cut through flowerettes into thin strips
                                        Cut stem into thin slices
                                        Cut stem in roll cut
                       Uncooked   Use only tip ends as dippers

Brussels Sprouts   Cooked   Cut into halves

Cabbage   Cooked   Mince or cut fine for salads
                                        Shred or grate
                                        Roll leaves around left-over meats
                       Uncooked   Mince, shred, or cut fine
                                        Form tulip, lily from the tip ends
                                          of the leaves

Carrot   Cooked   Cut into flower shape
                                        Cut to stand
                                        Use roll cut, slice, dice, or thin strips

	Uncooked	Grate
		Pencil cut
		Thin strips
		Cut into rose
Daikon		Try any cut you please—this vegetable is so versatile. It is the best medium for Fish Net Cut
Eggplant	Cooked	Slice in rounds
		Cut in strips
		Slice lengthwise
		Dice
	Uncooked	Use as vase with or without stenciled design
Fennel	Uncooked	Lotus cut
Jicama	Uncooked	Slice
		Cut into strips
		Cut into crescents
		Bird cut
		Fish cut
Leek	Uncooked	Flower cut
		Use green tops for flavoring
Melons		Make into flower rose using outside skin

		Make into basket
		Serve melon balls on skewers
		Make into sunflower or rose
Melon, Watermelon		Use long melon and fashion into whale
		Use round melon and create turkey
Melon, Winter Melon	Cooked	Use as container for meal (steamed)
		Put your meat and vegetables, stock, into cavity (use steamer-type)
Okra	Cooked	Slice in rounds
		Diagonal cut
Onion, Green	Cooked	Slice
	Uncooked	Use in flower cut
Onion, Dry (Yellow, White, Purple)	Cooked	Lotus cut
		Thin slice in rings
		Slice into quarters
	Uncooked	Lotus cut
Parsley		Mince and use as edging for other vegetables
		Use as a sprig of color

Potato	Cooked	Use the roll cut, steam
		After baking, use the roll cut, add condiments
	Uncooked	Make into flower
		Use small potatoes and make into pinecones
Pumpkin	Cooked	Steam and use as container
	Uncooked	Make into vase—with or without pattern (tape your own stencil on pumpkin and cut around the design)
Radish, Red	Uncooked	Experiment! Work with color contrast
Rutabaga	Cooked	Cut into fourths
		Diagonal cut
		Slice
	Uncooked	Flower cut
		Use as sturdy base to insert appetizers
Spinach	Cooked	Use plant as a whole and quickly boil. Place stem ends down; gradually turn tops over. Remove from heat when cooked and rinse under cold water to retain color.
	Uncooked	Fashion different leaf shapes
		Chop into bite-sizes for salad

Sunchoke (Jerusalem Artichoke)	Cooked	Slice into rounds
		Cut into strips
	Uncooked	Flower cut
		Bird cut
		Fish cut
		Rabbit cut
Tomato	Cooked	Cut in half and broil
	Uncooked	Peel and make rose of peel
		Make into cup or basket for filling
		Make into flower
		Make into wedges
		Make into bird Use a *firm* tomato
		Make into mushroom for borders
Turnip	Cooked	Dice
		Slice
	Uncooked	Make into daffodil, daisy
Zucchini	Cooked	Slice into rounds
		Slice lengthwise into fingers
		Roll cut
	Uncooked	Steam and make into boat
		Use flower cutter for shape
		Cut into strips

An apology is made to the vegetables not listed. Those selected are probably the vegetables found in most kitchens. To add interest through contrast to your menu, attempt at each meal to present a different cut. Soon you will discover which cut you prefer to give the best effect for each recipe. Speed will come as you familiarize yourself with the various cuts.

GLOSSARY OF JAPANESE TERMS

Ainu   a people of Japan that are now confined to living in the northernmost part of the island of Hokkaido

chorishi   person who puts food together

daikon   large white radish

dashi   soup stock

gokun   the five senses

hangetsu-giri   a crescent cut

Hiyo Setsu No Mon   name of restaurant, Ice and Snow Gate

hōchō   knife

hōchō-shiki   knife demonstration

icho-giri   round slice that has been quartered

itamae   title given to a master chef

kami   to free the essence

kampo   natural foods used as medicine

katsura-muki   to cut in a very thin sheet

kikka-kabu   cut like a chrysanthemum

mijin-giri   to mince cut

mirin   sweet Japanese rice wine

mono no aware   pure awareness

morimono   stacked pieces

mukimono   shaped pieces

nanami-giri   diagonal cut

on	an intrinsic gift
onishime	cooked vegetables, cut in different shapes
rangiri	roll cut
Samurai	warriors
sashimi	sliced raw fish
sengiri	thin strip cut
shun	awareness to seasonal changes and foods
soba	wheat noodle
suribachi	stringed bowl with wooden pestel
suwaru	manner of sitting
tanzaku	rectangular cut
tokonoma	recessed opening in Japanese home for the hanging of scrolls
wa-giri	round slice

Pronunciation of Japanese Words

a   above

e   end

i   ink

o   own

u   hue

"Salvador Deli"

Imagination gone berserk—the lowly carrot, with green pepper fronds transport you to islands far away. The papaya halves with wedges of lemon and lime speak of warm vacation lands.

Visual image only.

160